A BOOK OF PRAYERS AND BLESSINGS

A Book of Prayers and Blessings

Edited by Brian Magee, C.M.

Servant Publications
Ann Arbor, Michigan

Published in 1992 in the United States of America by
Servant Publications
P.O. Box 8617
Ann Arbor, Michigan 48107

First published in 1989 in Ireland by Veritas Publications
7-8 Lower Abbey Street
Dublin 1, Ireland

Printed with ecclesiastical approval

Acknowledgments
Excerpts from the English translation of the *Rite of Baptism for
Children* © 1969, International Committee on English in the
Liturgy, Inc. (ICEL); excerpts from the English translation of
The Roman Missal © 1973, ICEL; excerpts from the English
translation and original texts and pastoral notes from *Pastoral
Care of the Sick: Rites of Anointing and Viaticum* © 1982, ICEL;
the English translation of *Sub Tuum Praesidium* from *A Book of
Prayers* © 1982, ICEL; excerpts from the English translation
of and original texts from the *Order of Christian Funerals* ©
1985, ICEL. All rights reserved. Excerpts taken from the
Jerusalem Bible, published and copyright 1985 by Darton,
Longman and Todd Ltd. and Doubleday & Co Inc., used by
permission of the publishers. Extracts from *The Psalms: A New
Translation,* A.P. Watt Ltd. on behalf of the Grail, England.

Cover design by Michael Andaloro

92 93 94 95 96 10 9 8 7 6 5 4 3 2 1

Printed in the United States of America

ISBN 0-89283-761-6

Library of Congress Cataloging-in-Publication Data

Veritas book of blessing prayers.
    A book of prayers and blessings / edited by Brian Magee.
        p.   cm.
    Originally published: The Veritas book of prayers and blessings.
   Dublin, Ireland: Veritas Publications, 1989.
    Includes index.
    ISBN 0-89283-761-6: $8.99 (tent.)
    1. Benediction 2. Catholic Church — Customs and practices. 3.
Catholic Church — Prayer-books and devotions —English.
    I. Magee, Brian, C.M.   II. Title.
BX2048.B5V47   1992
242' .802 — dc20

CONTENTS

INTRODUCTION

Among the sacramentals in the life of the faithful the use of blessings has always been important. They are prayers in praise of God which help to dispose the faithful for the fruitful use of the sacraments. The Second Vatican Council wished that the faithful should be able to participate in them intelligently, actively, and easily; and that these blessings should be suited to contemporary situations. No longer would many blessings be reserved, but only a few such would be the prerogative of bishops. *(Constitution on the Liturgy, 79)*

PRAISE GOD FROM WHOM ALL BLESSINGS FLOW

God is the source of all blessings, and in particular he has blessed us in Jesus Christ. In the gospel we see Jesus blessing those who came to him, and offering prayers of blessing to his Father. He sent the Holy Spirit that we might be able to express praise, blessing and thanksgiving. In the Jewish liturgy the blessing or *berakah* became a characteristic form of prayer. Blessing formulas, with a usual beginning of 'Blessed are you, Lord, our God, king of the universe', developed for every kind of occasion. The Eucharistic Prayer of the Church developed from these forms.

MEANING OF BLESSING

We use the term blessing in two ways. Firstly, we bless and praise God for the gifts he has given to us, for his goodness shown to us. Secondly, we ask God to bless persons or things we use, that is to continue to show his goodness to us. When we ask God to bless the things we use we are praising him for the gift of these things, and pledging ourselves to use them in the right manner. When we praise God, from whom all blessings flow, we acknowledge his power to help us in our weakness, we remember his faithfulness to the covenant, and extol his majesty and goodness. The use of Sacred Scripture

1

in blessings calls to mind the whole story of God's favours to his people, and reminds us that all blessings refer to God.

BLESSINGS IN THE LIFE OF THE CHURCH

Throughout its history the Church has celebrated blessings praising God and imploring divine grace at important moments in the lives of its members. Blessings have been called down upon objects and places used by the faithful or related to the sacramental and devotional life of the Church. These blessings relate to those who use these things and to the manner in which they use them. They help us to sanctify the various activities of our human life. In the Irish tradition the prayer of blessing was on the lips of the people at every occasion in the day. Again the use of Sacred Scripture enlivens our faith and helps us to bring the proper dispositions for receiving God's blessing at these particular moments.

IN THE EARLY CHURCH

From the very beginning of the Church, formulas for blessing were preserved. The *Apostolic Tradition* of Hippolytus, from the early third century includes blessings at Mass for oil, cheese and olives, bread, new fruits and evening lights. In the later sacramentaries of Rome, Gaul and Spain, blessings are found for these as well as for church vessels and vestments, for buildings, and fruits of the harvest. In the later middle ages these blessings increased in number and were gathered into special books called *rituals*. As these sometimes contained superstitious elements they were in need of reform by the Council of Trent.

THE TRIDENTINE RITUAL

Pope Paul V published *The Roman Ritual* of 1614. It contained some thirty official blessings for the local church presided over by the bishop or parish priest. These were mainly of things, such as houses, ships and foodstuffs. Later editions added more blessings, and others were approved for religious congregations. The *Ritual* made provision for the addition of blessings for local needs and situations.

THE BOOK OF BLESSINGS

In response to the decrees of the Second Vatican Council the new *Book of Blessings* was published in Latin in 1984 and the official English translation has been published by ICEL. This new ritual stresses the communal celebration of liturgical functions, calling for the participation of at least some of the faithful on the occasion of a blessing. The ministry of blessing involves a particular exercise of the priesthood of Christ, and whenever a priest or deacon is present the office of presiding should be left to him. But lay persons, in virtue of the universal priesthood, may celebrate certain blessings in virtue of their office, for example, parents on behalf of their children. We are all called to pray for God's blessings on each other. The traditional prayers and blessings are essentially prayers for the laity. But we are always to ensure that the proper understanding of a blessing does not allow superstition or shallow credulity to take the place of genuine faith.

THE CELEBRATION OF BLESSINGS

The blessings are designed to be used with greater or lesser solemnity according to the circumstances of time and place, and the resources of the community. Each can be adapted by the minister to fit particular needs.

FORM OF BLESSING

The order of the blessing generally has the form of:

1. a) Greeting
   b) Introduction
2. Proclamation of the Word of God
3. Intercessions and Prayers
4. Blessing and Dismissal

1. Greeting and Introduction

The introduction contains the greeting, forms of which are given, followed by the celebrant's words of explanation. If the presider at a communal celebration is a priest or deacon he should wear an alb and white stole, or one of the colour of the day or season.

2. Proclamation of the Word of God

The Scripture readings vary in form and length, and can be expanded by the addition of a short homily.

3. Intercession and Prayers

The intercessions and prayers praise and bless God for his goodness, and ask for his help and blessing in the particular circumstance.

4. Blessing and Dismissal

Formulas for blessing are given in a general collection (pp. 5-7) and also in individual places.

To these should be added the outward sign or gesture, such as the raising or joining of hands, the laying on of hands, the sign of the cross, the sprinkling with holy water, the anointing with blessed oil, and incensation.

The following selection of greetings and blessings may be used at choice on the occasion of the celebration of a blessing. Priests and deacons would use the 'you' form, lay people the 'us' form, as illustrated in Blessing 1 and 2, and in Greeting 1.

Greetings

1. The grace of our Lord Jesus Christ and the love of God and the fellowship of the Holy Spirit be with you all.
   or
   The grace of our Lord Jesus Christ and the love of God and the fellowship of the Holy Spirit be with us all.

2. The grace and peace of God our Father and the Lord Jesus Christ be with you.

3. The grace of our Lord Jesus Christ be with you all.

4. The Lord be with you.

Blessings

1. May almighty God bless you,
   the Father, and the Son, ✶ and the Holy Spirit.
   R AMEN.

2. May the almighty and merciful God bless and protect us,
   the Father, and the Son, ✶ and the Holy Spirit.
   R AMEN.

3. May the peace of God
   which is beyond all understanding
   keep your hearts and minds
   in the knowledge and love of God
   and of his Son, our Lord Jesus Christ.
   R AMEN.
   May almighty God bless you,
   the Father, and the Son, ✶ and the Holy Spirit.
   R AMEN.

4. May God bless you with every good gift from on high.
   May he keep you pure and holy in his sight at all times.
   May he bestow the riches of his grace upon you,
   bring you the good news of salvation,
   and always fill you with love for all.
   R AMEN.
   May almighty God bless you,
   the Father, and the Son, ✠ and the Holy Spirit.
   R AMEN.

5. Go forth into the world in peace;
   be of good courage;
   hold fast to that which is good;
   render to no one evil for evil;
   strengthen the faint-hearted; support the weak;
   help the afflicted; honour each person;
   love and serve the Lord, rejoicing in the power of the Holy
   Spirit.
   And may the blessing of almighty God,
   the Father, the Son, ✠ and the Holy Spirit
   come upon you, and remain with you for ever.
   R AMEN.

6. May the Lord bless you,
   and protect you from all evil,
   and bring you to everlasting life.
   R AMEN.

7. May the Lord bless you and keep you.
   R AMEN.
   May his face shine upon you,
   and be gracious to you.
   R AMEN.
   May he look upon you with kindness,
   and give you his peace.
   R AMEN.
   May almighty God bless you,
   the Father, and the Son, ✠ and the Holy Spirit.
   R AMEN.

8. May the blessing of God almighty,
   the Father, and the Son, ✠ and the Holy Spirit,

rest upon you and upon your homes,
this day and evermore.
R AMEN.

9. May the Lord bless us,
   protect us from all evil,
   and bring us to everlasting life.
   R AMEN.

10. Father,
    look kindly upon your children who put their trust in you;
    bless them and keep them from all harm,
    strengthen them against the attacks of the devil.
    May they never offend you
    but seek to love you in all they do.
    We ask this through Christ our Lord.
    R AMEN.

AN ADDICT
(OF DRUGS, ALCOHOL, GAMBLING ETC.)

Our Lord Jesus Christ came to bring us the glorious
liberty of the children of God. Let us pray for that
freedom in our lives, using St Paul's prayer.

This, then, is what I pray, kneeling before the
    Father,
from whom every fatherhood in heaven or on earth,
    takes its name.
In the abundance of his glory
may he, through his Spirit, enable you
to grow firm in power with regard to your inner
    self,
so that Christ may live in your hearts through faith,
and then, planted in love and built on love,
with all God's holy people you will have the strength
to grasp the breadth and the length, the height and
    the depth;
so that, knowing the love of Christ, which is beyond
    knowledge,
you may be filled with the utter fullness of God.
Glory be to him
whose power, working in us,
can do infinitely more than we can ask or imagine;
glory be to him
from generation to generation in the Church
and in Christ Jesus for ever and ever. AMEN.

Ephesians 3:15-21

Let us pray:

Lord, open our hearts to receive your gift of grace,
the love that releases us from our bondage and gives
    us freedom:

freedom from cares and worries that stifle our
    happiness;
freedom from sins that cling to us, and to which we
    cling;
freedom from all that prevents our becoming what
    we can be and ought to be.
So bring us, Lord, to the experience of life more
    abundant,
through Jesus Christ our Lord. AMEN.

May the peace of God, which passes all
    understanding,
keep your heart and mind in the knowledge and
    love of God,
and of his Son Jesus Christ our Lord;
and the blessing of almighty God,
the Father, and the Son, ✳ and the Holy Spirit,
be upon you, and remain with you always.
AMEN.

CEREMONY OF THANKSGIVING
FOR AN ADOPTED CHILD

When a child who has already been baptised is being adopted, the adoptive parents may wish to celebrate the occasion with the ceremony which follows. The ceremony may take place at some convenient time after the adoptive parents have become the legal parents. In the ceremony the parents thank God for the gift of the child, commit themselves to rearing it in the faith, and pray for the guidance and strength of the Holy Spirit.

The ceremony may take place in the home of the parents, the parish church or in any other suitable place.

Sponsors may be appointed, if in practice the original godparents are unable to fulfil their role. (The term 'godparent' refers to the person who represents the Church at the baptism ceremony, and undertakes to help the parents bring up the child in the faith. In the case of adoption the godparents will at times be unknown and not in a position to fulfil their role. In such cases parents may choose one or two 'sponsors' who will be ready, should the situation arise, to help bring up the child to profess the faith).

Friends, relatives and representatives of the local community may gather with the parents and any other member of the household.

A candle is lighted.

OPENING ADDRESS

Priest: **In the name of the Father, and of the Son and of the Holy Spirit.**

All: **Amen.**

Priest: **My dear friends, we have come together today to share the joy of N and N as they thank God for the gift of this child. Through baptism we are, all of us, the adopted children of God. With confidence, therefore, we gather to pray that everything we do will be in accordance with his will.**

N and N (addressing the parents), God has given you the privilege of welcoming N (naming the child) into your home and raising him/her in the faith. May the Spirit be with you to guide you and to strengthen you as you take upon yourselves the responsibilities of Christian parents.

SCRIPTURE READING

Priest: Let us now together welcome God's word.
All: Lord, it is your face that we seek.
Hide not your face from us. AMEN.

Any appropriate reading may be used, e.g.

Mark 10:13-16

People brought young children to Jesus that he might touch them. The disciples rebuked them. When Jesus saw this he was greatly displeased, and he said to them: 'Leave the little children to come to me, and do not forbid them. For of such is the Kingdom of God. Amen I say to you, whosoever does not receive the Kingdom of God like a little child shall never enter it.' Then he embraced them, and laid his hands upon them, and blessed them.

A short homily may follow

DECLARATION OF ACCEPTANCE

Priest: N and N (addressing the parents), in adopting N (naming the child) you are accepting the responsibility of raising him/her in the faith of the Church. It will be your duty and privilege to help him/her to grow up in the knowledge, love and grace of God. Are you prepared to take on this responsibility?

Parents: **We are.**

RENEWAL OF CHRISTIAN COMMITMENT

Priest: **As you declare your acceptance of this responsibility, I invite you to renew your Christian commitment.**

He addresses the parents and sponsors as follows, or in the words of the Rite of Baptism for Children given below:

Priest: **Do you believe in God the Father Almighty?**

R We do, and we acknowledge him to be the source of all life. We believe that he chose each one of us before the foundation of the world, and destined us in love to be his children.

Priest: **Do you believe in God the Son?**

R We do. We believe that Jesus Christ, the risen Lord, is alive and with us all days even to the end of the world.

Priest: **Do you believe in God the Holy Spirit?**

R We do. We believe that he is with his Church, and with each one of us, guiding us, strengthening us, and keeping us always in the Father's love.

Priest: **Do you resolve to hand on your faith to this child, and to remain true to that faith until death?**

12

R   We do. We resolve to be true to Christ in our family life, in our place of work, and in our moments of leisure. We resolve to be people of prayer, and to make the living God the centre of our lives. We resolve to give witness to our faith by the way we live, and to radiate the joy of the Lord in our daily lives. We resolve to reject violence in all its forms, and to be apostles of reconciliation and peace. We resolve to work for our community so that the poor will not be forgotten, nor those in need neglected. We resolve to raise our child in the faith, so that one day with the help of God he/she will make that faith his/her own, and treasure it to the end.

or, the priest may use the following from the Rite of Baptism of Children:

Priest: Do you reject Satan?
R   I do.

Priest: And all his works?
R   I do.

Priest: And all his empty promises?
R   I do.

Priest: Do you believe in God, the Father Almighty, creator of heaven and earth?
R   I do.

Priest: Do you believe in Jesus Christ, his only Son, our Lord, who was born of the Virgin Mary, was crucified, died, and was buried,

	rose from the dead, and is now seated at the right hand of the Father?
R	I do.
Priest:	Do you believe in the Holy Spirit, the holy Catholic Church, the communion of saints, the forgiveness of sins, the resurrection of the body, and the life everlasting?
R	I do.
Priest:	This is our faith. This is the faith of the Church. We are proud to profess it, in Christ Jesus our Lord.
All:	AMEN.

THE SIGNING

Priest: **N** (addressing the child), **with joy we welcome you into this community of N** (naming the parish or community) **and we sign you with the mark of our Saviour, to whom you belong since your baptism.**

The priest signs the child on the forehead in silence with the sign of the Cross, then invites the parents and sponsors to do the same.

CEREMONY OF THE LIGHTED CANDLE

Handing the lighted candle to the parents the priest says:

Receive this burning light
as a sign of the faith in which N has been baptised.
Help him/her by the example of your own lives to grow in that faith

14

until the day when he/she will see the Lord
face to face in the light of heaven.

PRAYER OF PARENTS (TOGETHER)

God our Father
with joy we welcome N into our home,
with joy we take him/her to our hearts.
Send us the help of your Spirit
so that in raising our child
we will always know what to do
and have the strength to do it.
We ask this through Christ our Lord.

R   AMEN.

Priest: May God who has begun this good work
bring it to perfection.
R   AMEN.

PRAYER OF PARTICIPANTS

Priest: Let us turn to our Saviour who was himself
entrusted by his heavenly Father to the care
of Mary and Joseph and pray for N, his/her
parents, and the whole Church:

The parents, sponsors and people present may
pray in turn in these or similar words:

Lord Jesus, may N find love, happiness and
care in his/her new home. May he/she grow
up to love the Lord God with all his/her
heart, and his/her neighbour as himself/
herself. Lord hear our prayer.

15

R   Lord hear our prayer.

Lord Jesus, may N and N, together with N their child, grow into a happy family, and always be united in their faith, their hope and their love. Lord hear our prayer. R

Lord Jesus, may N and N find happiness in each other, and be blessed in their child. Lord hear our prayer. R

Lord Jesus, may your peace ever dwell in this (their) home, may the angels of God protect it, and may the holy family of Nazareth be its model and inspiration. Lord hear our prayer. R

Lord Jesus, inspire us all to be living examples of the faith to N and to one another. Lord hear our prayer. R

Lord Jesus, look with kindness on those who have given this child for adoption, and fill their hearts with love of you. Lord hear our prayer. R

Lord Jesus, may all who are engaged in adoption work have the wisdom to make good decisions, and the kindness and understanding which their work requires. Lord hear our prayer. R

Lord Jesus, may we all see long and happy days, and be united one day in the fellowship of heaven. Lord hear our prayer. R

Priest:	Together, as adopted children of our common Father, let us pray:
All:	Our Father,...

Priest:	God our Father, hear our prayers and in your love make up for whatever is lacking in our lives. We ask this through Christ our Lord.
R	AMEN.

Priest:	Holy Mary
R	Pray for us.

Priest:	Saint N (naming the child's patron):
R	Pray for us.

BLESSING OF PARENTS

Priest:	Almighty God, giver of life, look with favour on N and N. May they be blessed in their child and ever grow closer in their love for each other. May they always know the joy of your help and the strength of your presence. And when life is over may they be united for ever where parting is no more in the kingdom of your love. We ask this through Christ our Lord.
R	AMEN.

BLESSING OF ALL PRESENT

Priest: **May the Father of love send his peace on all who are gathered here today. And may almighty God bless you, the Father, and the Son, ✠ and the Holy Spirit.**

R **AMEN**.

DEDICATION TO MARY

(Appropriately, the dedication may take place on another occasion, e.g. at a shrine of Mary.)

Priest: **Let us turn to Mary, our Mother, and place N under her protection** (a medal of the Blessed Virgin may be placed on the child):

For a girl:

**O Mary, mother of God and our mother,
we dedicate this child to your loving care.
Today we choose you for her mother, guide and friend.
May she always live devoted to you and desire, say and do only what is pleasing to you.
O most tender and loving mother,
we beg you through the infinite merits of Jesus, your divine Son,
to regard her at all times among the children especially dear to you,**

18

and to obtain for her the grace of a holy life,
a life of goodness, purity and love,
offered to God in thanksgiving and praise.
Be present with her at all times, O Blessed Virgin Mary,
and especially at the hour of her death.
Then, Mary, pray for her and protect her from the enemy of her soul.
Guide her safely into the presence of our holy Redeemer
to be happy for ever in the company of all the angels and saints in Heaven.
AMEN.

For a boy:

O Mary, mother of God and our mother,
we dedicate this child to your loving care.
Today we choose you for his mother, guide and friend.
May he always live devoted to you
and desire, say and do only what is pleasing to you.
O most tender and loving mother,
we beg you through the infinite merits of Jesus, your divine Son,
to regard him at all times among the children especially dear to you,
and to obtain for him the grace of a holy life,

a life of goodness, purity and love,
offered to God in thanksgiving and
praise.
Be present with him at all times, O
Blessed Virgin Mary,
and especially at the hour of his death.
Then, Mary, pray for him and protect
him from the enemy of his soul.
Guide him safely into the presence of
our holy Redeemer
to be happy for ever in the company of
all the angels and saints in Heaven.

Priest: **Let us bless the Lord.**
R **Thanks be to God.**

All present may congratulate the parents and
greet the child.

ADVENT WREATH

Today we begin preparing to celebrate, with hope-filled joy, the coming of the Lord at Christmas. We ask God's blessing on this wreath of evergreens.

The Word was the real light
that gives light to everyone;
he was coming into the world.
from his fullness, we have, all of us, received.

John 1:9.16

Let us pray:

Father, all powerful Lord of Light, bless our wreath of evergreens with its candles.

May our Advent be a time of preparation. Help us reflect on the power of light to dispel darkness in our world and in our lives. Touch our hearts with the warmth of your love. May the increasing light of these candles brighten our minds and hearts to be steadfast in faith, joyful in hope and untiring in love, so that we are ready, again to receive in true peace, Jesus, the Light of the World, our Lord and Saviour. AMEN.

AIRCRAFT

We read in the Gospel according to Matthew:

I am telling you not to worry about your life
and what you are to eat,
nor about your body and what you are to wear.
Look at the birds in the sky!
They do not sow or reap or gather into barns;
yet your heavenly Father feeds them
Are you not worth much more than they are?
Set your hearts on his kingdom first, and on his
      righteousness,
and all these other things will be given you as well.

Matthew 6:25.26.33

Responsorial Psalm   *Ps 139*

R   IF I CLIMB THE HEAVENS, O LORD, YOU ARE THERE.

1. O Lord, you search me and you know me,
      you know my resting and my rising,
      you discern my purpose from afar.
      You mark when I walk or lie down,
      all my ways lie open to you. R

2. O where can I go from your spirit,
      or where can I flee from your face?
      If I climb the heavens you are there.
      If I lie in the grave you are there. R

3. If I take the wings of the dawn
      and dwell at the sea's furthest end,
      even there your hand would lead me,
      your right hand would hold me fast. R

Let us pray:

Lord God,
you have made all creatures for your own glory,
and placed the things of creation at our service.
Bless this machine* built for air travel,
that it may serve,
without loss or danger,
for spreading ever more widely
the praise and glory of your name,
and for the quicker despatch of the world's affairs.
May all who use it lift their hearts and minds to heaven
    above,
where you live and reign for ever and ever.
AMEN.

* This prayer may be used in the plural for the
blessing of a fleet.

ALCOHOL ADDICTION

Jesus said:

Be compassionate just as your Father is compassionate. Do not judge and you will not be judged; do not condemn, and you will not be condemned; forgive, and you will be forgiven. Give, and there will be gifts for you: a full measure, pressed down, shaken together, and running over, will be poured into your lap; because the standard you use will be the standard used for you.

Luke 6:37-38

Let us pray:

Compassionate God,
help us to understand alcoholism and the effect alcohol has on the individual who is suffering.

Help us to recognise that alcoholism is a family disease and that other family members also need our help, support and encouragement.

Give us the gift of accepting the alcoholic even while we pray for the grace of heartfelt repentance and lasting changes for him.

Give us the strength to see behind the tortured facade the true person, who is your child in need.

Help us to avoid being intolerant, judgmental, moralistic and impatient.

We ask this through Christ our Lord.

God grant us the serenity to accept the things we cannot change, courage to change the things we can,
and the wisdom to know the difference.

AMEN.

ANIMALS 1

Animals help us in so many ways, enhance and enrich our lives and give us their loyalty and friendship. While science has benefited us extensively and has removed so much pain from our lives, it has sadly been perverted to increase the burden of suffering on animals. We must acknowledge that we have no right to visit our afflictions upon innocent animals. Still less must we inflict upon them diseases, unnatural to them, which arise from our sinfulness and self-indulgence, nor are they to be made the victims of our greed, vanity and curiosity.

We read in scripture:

The upright has compassion on his animals, but the heart of the wicked is ruthless.   *Proverbs 12:10*

Then God said to Noah: Behold, I establish my covenant with you and your descendants after you, and with every living creature that is with you, the birds, the cattle, and every beast of the earth with you, as many as came out of the ark.   *Genesis 9:9-10*

Let us pray:

Eternal Father, at the very dawn of human history you have given, through Noah, your protecting covenant to all animals as well as to us. We intercede, therefore, for our friends the animals and their welfare.

Inspired by the Gospel message of mercy, given us by your Divine Son, may all of us use our unique gifts of reason to protect these less privileged creatures which share this planet with us. We ask this through Christ our Lord.

AMEN.

ANIMALS 2

The Psalmist writes:

Let everything that lives and that breathes
give praise to the Lord.
Alleluia   *Psalm 150:6*

Let us pray:

Eternal God,
in your love you create all things,
and within your great purpose
provide every kind of animal.
May the whole of creation rejoice in you,
and every creature experience the joy and wonder
of the life for which you have made it.
Give to all your people an attitude
of care and consideration for animals,
that we may honour you, the creator,
through Jesus Christ our Lord.
AMEN.

ANNIVERSARY/JUBILEE

We read in the Book of Ecclesiasticus:

Bless the God of all things,
the doer of great deeds everywhere,
who has exalted our days from the womb
and acted towards us in his mercy.
May he grant us cheerful hearts
and bring peace in our time,
in Israel for ages on ages,
may his mercy be faithfully with us,
may he redeem us in our time.

50:24-26

Responsorial Psalm   *Ps 137:1-5*

R   I THANK YOU, LORD, FOR YOUR FAITHFULNESS
AND LOVE.

1. I thank you, Lord, with all my heart,
   you have heard the words of my mouth.
   Before the angels I will bless you.
   I will adore before your holy temple. R

2. I thank you for your faithfulness and love
   which excel all we ever knew of you.
   On the day I called, you answered;
   you increased the strength of my soul. R

3. All earth's kings shall thank you
   when they hear the words of your mouth.
   They shall sing of the Lord's ways:
   'How great is the glory of the Lord!' R

27

A reading from the holy Gospel according to Matthew
7:7-11

Jesus said to his disciples: 'Ask, and it will be given to you; search, and you will find; knock, and the door will be opened to you. For the one who asks always receives; the one who searches always finds; the one who knocks will always have the door opened to him. Is there a man among you who would hand his son a stone when he asked for bread? Or would hand him a snake when he asked for a fish? If you, then, who are evil, know how to give your children what is good, how much more will your Father in heaven give good things to those who ask him!'

This is an occasion for thanksgiving for the graces given over the past years. It is also perhaps an occasion of regret for the failures and mistakes of that period. But it is also one of healing and reconciliation, with dedication anew for the tasks ahead. Let us bless and thank the Lord:

Blessed are you, Lord of the times and seasons,
we thank you for your gift of time:
for the days past in which your favour has rested
    upon us.
Look not on our past weakness but give us the
    strength to go forward in hope and trust.

Let us pray:

WEDDING ANNIVERSARY

Living God,
you created man and woman
to love each other

in the bond of marriage.
Bless and strengthen N and N,
May their marriage become an increasingly more
    perfect sign of the union between Christ and
    his Church.
We ask this through Christ our Lord. AMEN.

Silver wedding anniversary

Father,
you have blessed and sustained N and N,
in the bond of marriage.
Continue to increase their love
throughout the joys of their married life,
and help them to grow in holiness all their days.
We ask this through Christ our Lord. AMEN.

Golden wedding anniversary

God, our Father,
bless N and N,
We thank you for their long and happy marriage
(for the children they have brought into the world)
and for all the good they have done.
As you blessed the love of their youth,
continue to bless their life together
with gifts of peace and joy.
We ask this through Christ our Lord. AMEN.

God of faithfulness,
today N comes to give you thanks
and to rededicate that gift first received from you.
We thank you for the loving service
that he/she has given to your people.
Renew that love within him/her
that in the years to come greater glory
may be given to your holy name.
We ask this through Christ our Lord. AMEN.

May almighty God bless you,
the Father, and the Son, ✠ and the Holy Spirit.
AMEN.

THE BEDRIDDEN

Listen to God's promise —
I will not leave you or desert you.

Joshua 1:5

Let us pray:

Lord of mercy and of love,
you know the weakness and the fears of your
        servants:
In your mercy, give strength to the bedridden,
who do not enjoy the freedom of walking about,
and are dependent on others for so much.
When they are frustrated, give them courage,
and when in despair, give them hope.
May they always know your presence,
and find purpose and meaning in life
and rejoice in your love;
through Jesus Christ our Lord.
AMEN.

May the God of hope
fill you with all joy and peace
in believing,
so that by the power of the Holy Spirit
you may abound in hope.

In this time of sorrow let us pray for strength and
peace.
We listen first to the Lord's words of
encouragement:

Jesus said to his disciples:
'Do not let your hearts be troubled.
You trust in God, trust also in me.
In my Father's house there are many places to live
in;
otherwise I would have told you.
I am going now to prepare a place for you,
and after I have gone and prepared you a place,
I shall return to take you to myself,
so that you may be with me
where I am.'   *John 14:1-3*

Let us pray:

God, loving Father,
be close to those who are mourning the loss of one
so dear to them.
Heal the pain they now suffer,
lighten their darkness,
and scatter the doubts that their grief brings.
Let the remembrance
of how your Son Jesus wept at the death of Lazarus
his friend be a consolation to them at this time.
May they feel Christ's healing power come to them
in their pain and distress.
Give them the strength to keep on going forward
with faith as their consolation
and eternal life as their hope.

Grant everlasting rest and peace to the one they
loved.

May they keep the memory of their joy in him/her
ever fresh.

Grant that we may all be gathered together again in
the joy of your Kingdom with the Virgin Mary
and all the saints.

We ask this through Christ our Lord. Amen.

May almighty God bless you,

the Father, and the Son, ✠ and the Holy Spirit.
AMEN.

The Lord Jesus applied to himself the words of
     Isaiah:
The Spirit of Lord Yahweh is on me.
  for Yahweh has anointed me.
  He has sent me to bring the news to the afflicted,
  to soothe the broken-hearted,
  to proclaim liberty to captives,
  release to those in prison.   *Isaiah 61:1-2*

Let us pray:

We ask you, loving Lord, to look with compassion
     on these your children who are sorrowing over
     the death of N.
Comfort them and all who mourn, provide for those
     who grieve,
  give them for ashes a garland,
  for mourning-dress the oil of gladness,
  for despondency, festal attire;
  the oil of gladness instead of mourning,
  and a garment of praise instead of the spirit of
     despair,
  so that they may be oaks of righteousness,
  a planting of the Lord for the display of his
     splendour.   *Isaiah 61:1-3*

THOSE BEREAVED BY SUICIDE

Jesus said to his disciples:

Do not let your hearts be troubled.
Trust in God still, and trust in me.
There are many rooms in my Father's house;
if there were not, I should have told you.

John 14:1-2

With faith in the word of Jesus let us pray: Lord in
    your mercy,
R HEAR OUR PRAYER.

Give us a deeper faith and trust in our time of grief:
    Lord in your mercy,
R HEAR OUR PRAYER.

Give us strength to bear this tragic loss:
    Lord in your mercy,
R HEAR OUR PRAYER.

The faith of the dead is known to you alone, judge
    her/him kindly: Lord, in your mercy,
R HEAR OUR PRAYER.

Look on the faith of those who love her/him: Lord,
    in your mercy:
R HEAR OUR PRAYER.

Do not consider her/his sins, nor judge in our
    human way: Lord in your mercy,
R HEAR OUR PRAYER.

Grant peace to her/him, and to all who mourn this
    sudden death: Lord, in your mercy,
R HEAR OUR PRAYER.

Lord, our God,
you are always faithful and quick to show mercy.
Our brother/sister N
was suddenly taken from us.
Come swiftly to his/her aid,
have mercy on him/her,
and comfort his/her family and friends
by the power and protection of the cross.
We ask this through Christ our Lord.
AMEN.

May almighty God bless you, the Father, and the
    Son, ✠ and the Holy Spirit.
AMEN.

Let us pray:

Lord Jesus Christ,
You experienced our humanity, our joys, our sorrows,
our hopes, our disappointments. We ask your blessing
✠ upon our sisters and brothers who mourn the tragic
death of N. Give them your grace so that they may face
the future with courage and hope.

We make this prayer through Christ our Lord.
AMEN.

A BIRTHDAY BLESSING PRAYER

As we rejoice with N on this birthday, we thank God
for all the blessings of life, and pray for greater growth.

St Paul reminded his followers at Ephesus:

'If we live by the truth and in love,
we shall grow completely into Christ,
who is the head by whom the whole Body is fitted and
joined together, every joint adding its own strength,
for each individual part to work according to its
function. So the body grows until it has built itself
up in love.'
                                          Ephesians 4:15-16

So let us thank God for life and growth:
> The baptismal candle of the person celebrating the
> birthday may be lit and held.

Blessed are you, Lord God, giver of life and growth:
you have been with N to this day of his/her life;
may that life be always nourished by you.
R BLESSED BE GOD FOR EVER!

Blessed are you, Lord Jesus Christ,
living among us you grew in wisdom and age and
        grace;
may N grow in grace and knowledge of you.
R BLESSED BE GOD FOR EVER!

Blessed are you, Holy Spirit, Lord of love,
you have filled N with your sevenfold gifts;
may he/she live in truth and love.
R BLESSED BE GOD FOR EVER!

Lord God, we thank you for the years that are past
and for all the good achieved in them.
Guide and direct N in the years to come
with your protection, help and strength;
so that in the fullness of time
he/she may come to the eternal celebration of life.
We ask this through Christ our Lord.

AMEN.

BREAD

Bread may be blessed before sharing it. It may be blessed at the end of Mass or at any other gathering. It may be normal everyday bread, or specially made — perhaps a festive cake! If it is not possible that all receive a piece broken from the one cake, then it is good that as each person receives a piece, he/she breaks it and shares it with another and, in turn, receives from another. In Greece it is known as 'Antidoron'; in France it is 'Pain Bénit'; in Poland it is 'Oplatki'.

Blessed are you, Lord God of all creation!
Through your goodness we have this bread to share.
As it is formed of many grains united as one,
may we who share it be satisfied in body
and united in mind and heart.
As it is the work of many hands,
may we who share it work together
to share with all the world
your gifts of food for body and soul.
As we draw strength from it for living in your love,
may it fill us with thanksgiving for all the food we
    receive today;
may it protect us from sickness and sin;
may it free us from greed and fill us with joy
so that we may bless your glorious name for ever
    and ever.
AMEN.

PARTNER IN A BROKEN MARRIAGE

Jesus said:

In the world you will have hardship,
but be courageous:
I have conquered the world. *John 16:33*

Let us pray for God's blessing on N and N.
> (The singular will be used if the blessing is for
> one partner only.)

Merciful and loving God,
You created the companionship of man and woman,
wanting them to be happy.

For a woman

Stay close to N
as she begins to cope with loneliness and loss.
Judge her sense of failure with pity and compassion.
Give her the courage and faith she needs
to face the future with hope and reassurance.
May your grace help her
through bad times to better days
as she searches to do your will.
Remove all bitterness from her heart
and bring her to your deep peace.
We ask this through Christ our Lord. AMEN.

For a man

Stay close to N
as he begins to cope with loneliness and loss.
Judge his sense of failure with pity and compassion.
Give him the courage and faith he needs
to face the future with hope and reassurance.
May your grace help him
through bad times to better days
as he searches to do your will.
Remove all bitterness from his heart
and bring him to your deep peace.
We ask this through Christ our Lord. AMEN.

N, may almighty God bless you
the Father, and the Son, ✠ and the Holy Spirit.
AMEN.

The words of sacred scripture remind us:

My child, support your father in his old age,
do not grieve him during his life.
Even if his mind should fail, show him sympathy,
do not despise him in your health and strength;
for kindness to a father will not be forgotten
but will serve as reparation for your sins.
In the days of your affliction it will be remembered of
    you,
like frost in sunshine, your sins will melt away.

Ecclesiasticus 3:12-14

Let us pray:

Pour out your blessings, Lord,
upon your faithful servant.
Grant her patience and courage in her daily task.
Fill her with the gift of love
to strengthen her in the work to which you have
    called her.
Give her an understanding of your caring presence,
so that at all times she may confidently
place her trust in you.
Forgive her failures and weaknesses
so that she may experience your gift of peace in her
    life.
We ask this through Christ our Lord.

May almighty God bless you, the Father, and the
    Son, ✠ and the Holy Spirit. AMEN.

THOSE CARING FOR THE AGED 2

The Apostle Paul wrote to the Corinthians:

Blessed be the God and Father of our Lord Jesus Christ...
he supports us in every hardship so that we are able to
come to the support of others. *2 Corinthians 1:3-4*

Let us pray:

God of all love and strength,
Support your servants who care for the aged.
May they give courage and self-respect
to those who feel weak and helpless,
and joy and hope to the sad and lonely.
When their task seems hard and demanding,
fill them with a sense of your strength and love,
through Jesus Christ our Lord.
AMEN.

A WOMAN BEFORE CHILDBIRTH

In the name of the Father,
and of the Son,
and of the Holy Spirit.
AMEN.

Let us call to mind that our Lord, Jesus, is with us
as he promised he would always be.

> A reading may be chosen, for example:
> Mark 9:33-37 or 10:13-16
> Luke 1:39-45
> Ephesians 3:14-21
> Colossians 1:9-14 or 3:12-17
> 1 John 4:7-21 or 5:1-5

Lord Jesus Christ, you shared our human nature,
and began your earthly life in the womb of Mary.
Lord Jesus, we praise you.
R   LORD JESUS, WE BLESS YOU!

Lord Jesus Christ, you gave your mother Mary to
your people to be a mother to us.
Lord Jesus, we praise you.
R   LORD JESUS, WE BLESS YOU!

Lord Jesus Christ, you honoured Mary your
mother, and in honouring her, you honour all
women.
Lord Jesus, we praise you.
R   LORD JESUS, WE BLESS YOU!

God,
creator of life,
we thank you for N,
and for your everlasting love for her.
Fill her with joy at the wonder of this new life.
Grant this through Jesus Christ, our Lord.
R AMEN.

Oil (for example, olive oil) may be used in blessing:

Lord God almighty,
before you the hosts of angels stand in awe.
We ask you to bless and make holy this oil
which you have created.
Let this oil protect
and bring health in body and mind
to all who use it.
May we be filled with your blessings
and give thanks to you,
the living and true God,
through Christ our Lord.
R AMEN.

BLESSING

Father of blessings,
lay your gentle and powerful hand on N
and surround her with the assurance of your love.
Bless and protect her.
Give her a safe delivery.
Bring her child to birth in full health.
Bless and guide her in her life.
May her child grow in wisdom and age and grace
in your presence and before your people.
Grant this through Christ, our Lord.
R AMEN.

May God, the source of life, in his goodness support you always.
R AMEN.

May he strengthen you in your faithfulness, confirm you in your hope,
and gift you always with the power of love.
R AMEN.

May he be with you as you await the birth of your child.
R AMEN.

And may almighty God bless you:
the Father, the Son, ✠ and the Holy Spirit!
R AMEN.

FOR SAFETY IN CHILDBIRTH

We rejoice with Mary in the joy of new life.

My soul glorifies the Lord,
my spirit rejoices in God, my saviour.
He looks on his servant in her nothingness;
henceforth all ages will call me blessed.
The Almighty works marvels for me.
Holy his name.
His mercy is from age to age,
on those who fear him.

Luke 1:46-49

Let us pray:

Almighty God,
We ask you to bless and protect this mother
who comes to you now with her worries and fears.
Give her strength and courage
as she puts all her trust in you.
Grant patience to her in the days of
waiting.
Grant her a safe delivery,
and the grace of holy Baptism for her baby.
We make our prayer through Christ our Lord.
AMEN.

THE CHILDLESS

In a world that seems to value the gift of life so lightly
it can be hard for a couple without a child. As they see
their friends with their little ones they feel longing,
sadness, and the temptation to bitterness, envy and
resentment. It is hard to see being childless as a special
vocation and not a cross. Love of children can be
channelled through adoption, fosterage or care of the
handicapped.

'So I say to you: Ask and it will be given to you; search
and you will find; knock, and the door will be opened
to you. For everyone who asks receives; everyone who
searches, finds; everyone who knocks will have the door
opened.'   *Luke 11:9-11*

Let us pray: (for N and N)

God of mercy and compassion,
N and N thank you for your many blessings
and especially for their love
which has grown throughout their married life.
Hear their prayers for the crowning blessing of a
    child.
Help them to accept your will in their lives,
and let their love bring joy to the world.
May the peace and joy of Nazareth be always in
    their home
as they place all their trust in you.

We make our prayer through Christ our Lord.
    AMEN.

CHILDREN
(BY PARENTS)

The Gospel tells us that people brought little children to him, for him to lay his hands on them and pray. The disciples scolded them, but Jesus said, 'Let the little children alone, and do not stop them coming to me, for it is to such as these that the kingdom of heaven belongs'. Then he laid his hands on them. *Matthew 19:13-15*

Parents may make a blessing sign by laying hands on the child's head, or making the sign of the cross on the forehead or breast as at baptism, using any of the following words:

a) Blessed are you, Lord God,
giver of life and love;
we thank you for the gift of our children;
may they grow before you in wisdom and grace;
through Christ our Lord.
AMEN.

b) May the blessing of almighty God come upon
      you,
give you the fullness of his life,
and make you strong in faith, hope and love,
through the grace of our Lord Jesus Christ
in the fellowship of the Holy Spirit.
AMEN.

c) God has called you by your name,
may he make you always his.
Jesus Christ has paid for you with a great price,
may you remain faithful to his call;
the Holy Spirit dwells in you as in a temple,

may you be filled with his gifts;
and may you come to live with the Trinity
in the kingdom of unity and peace.
AMEN.

d) A birthday blessing
We bless you, heavenly Father,
as we celebrate the birthday of N.
We thank you for the gift of life,
for the blessings of these....years,
and for giving us this day of joy.
N, may God fill your heart with his peace,
keep you in his loving care,
and bring you safely through the years to come.
We ask this through Christ our Lord.
AMEN.

e) Blessing of an older child
Lord God, who gave life to us all,
We thank you for the joy N has given us,
and ask your forgiveness for our failures in love.
Grant N for whom we pray this day,
health and strength,
wisdom and understanding,
courage and responsibility.

N, may the Lord bless you and keep you. ✠
May his face shine upon you and be gracious to
    you.
May he look upon you with kindness and give you
    his peace.

THE CHILDREN OF SEPARATED PEOPLE

Jesus said: 'Let the little children alone, and do not stop them coming to me; for it is to such as these that the kingdom of heaven belongs'.

Matthew 19:14

Let us pray:

Lord,
in this time of separation,
when emotions are running high,
when parents are so involved in their own hurts,
and preoccupied with their own needs,
we bring their children to you.
We place them in your hands;
we ask you to hold them close to you,
to guide them and protect them,
to let them experience your peace,
so that they may grow strong in your love.
We ask this through Christ our Lord.
AMEN.

CHRISTIAN COMMITMENT

A reading from the holy Gospel according to John
1:35-38

As John stood with two of his disciples, Jesus passed, and John stared hard at him and said, 'Look, there is the lamb of God'. Hearing this, the two disciples followed Jesus. Jesus turned round, saw them following and said, 'What do you want?' They answered, 'Rabbi' — which means Teacher — 'Where do you live?' 'Come and see,' he replied; so they went and saw where he lived, and stayed with him the rest of that day.

Responsorial Psalm   *Ps 122*

R   I REJOICED WHEN I HEARD THEM SAY:
     LET US GO TO GOD'S HOUSE.

1.   I rejoiced when I heard them say:
     'Let us go to God's house.'
     And now our feet are standing
     within your gates, O Jerusalem. R

2.   Jerusalem is built as a city
     strongly compact.
     It is there that the tribes go up,
     the tribes of the Lord. R

3.   For Israel's law it is,
     there to praise the Lord's name.
     There were set the thrones of judgement
     of the house of David. R

Let us pray:

Lord Jesus Christ our desire is to seek you
and to love you with all our hearts.
We have committed ourselves to following you
who are the Way, the Truth and the Life.
Strengthen us to live for the example and teaching
of your life and death.
Teach us to love as you did
even to laying down our lives for our friends.
Help us as we carry the cross daily with you.
When we are weary and over-burdened
let us hear your promise of rest.
Be with us as we travel the pilgrim road
so that our hearts may ever burn with love and joy.
Stay with us as evening comes
and light our way to where you live and reign
with the Father and the Holy Spirit
now and for ever.
AMEN.

THE CHRISTMAS CANDLE

A reading from the prophet Isaiah   9:1.5

The people that walked in darkness
have seen a great light;
on those who live in a land of deep shadow
a light has shone.
For there is a child born for us,
a son given to us
and dominion is laid on his shoulders;
and this is the name they give him;
Wonder-Counsellor, Mighty-God,
Eternal-Father, Prince-of-Peace.

Let us pray:

We thank you, heavenly Father,
for bringing us together this holy night.

We thank you for sending your Son, Jesus Christ,
to be our light and hope on the way of life.

Bless us as we gather here
and bless this Christmas candle.
Let it remind us of Christ, the Light of the World.
As it shines in our window
let us remember the poor and homeless
and let our hearts open to all in need.

Bless all who are in any trouble this night
and let them know your care
through the prayers of the Blessed Virgin Mary and Saint
Joseph.

Bless our absent relatives and friends,
especially N.
Give eternal rest and peace to the dead,
may perpetual light shine on them
and especially on N.

A member of the family now lights the candle.

Then is said:

Word become flesh in the springtime, welcome indeed!
Child born in a winter stable, more than truly welcome!
Only Son of Mary, a hundred thousand praises be yours,
And may the blessed Lord of us all give you health!

BLESSING

May the kindness and love of God, our Saviour, be upon
us and all we love:
in the name of the Father, and of the Son, ✠ and of the
Holy Spirit. AMEN.

A CHRISTMAS MANGER 1

I bring you news of great joy,
a joy to be shared by the whole people.
Today a Saviour has been born to you;
he is Christ the Lord.

Luke 2:10-11

Let us pray:

Heavenly Father,
As we wonder and hesitate to believe, like the
shepherds of Bethlehem, fill our hearts with joy, as
we recognise in this helpless babe the revelation of
your love, a new radiant vision of your glory.

Filled with wonder at the nearness of our God in
Mary's newborn child, may we now offer him our
praise, worship and thanksgiving and give him the
love and loyalty of our hearts. AMEN.

A CHRISTMAS MANGER 2

Let us pray:

Father, you are Lord of heaven and earth.
You guide the stars; you have the whole world in
      your hands;
you take care of all your people.
We thank you for all your gifts of love;
here today we thank you in a special way for this
      manger
We thank you for those who made it and for those
      who erected it.
We thank you for leading us to praise you with the
      help of this
manger. We thank you most of all for the birth of your
      Son.

We pray, Father, that you bless this manger. ✠
May it inspire all who pass by with the memory of
      your love.
May it brighten the hearts of our people
and lighten their burden.
You have already done so much for us;
may the memory of this open our hearts to all the
      great things you still want to do for us.
May there always be room in our hearts for your
      Son, and for all your children in need.
Bless us with the peace the angels announced.
Teach us to recognise your Son as the shepherds
      did.
May the light of your word guide us to him,
as the star guided the wise men;
make us generous with the gifts you have given us,
just as the wise men were generous.

Teach us to ponder all these things in our hearts, as Mary did.

May we look forward with even greater joy to the day when Jesus will come again, so that the whole world may see the glory you have given him. He now lives and reigns with you and the Holy Spirit, one God, forever and ever. AMEN.

A CHURCH ORGAN

Music is integral to our worship, and we bless this organ, dedicating it to the work of praise. We are called to be a people of praise; to give thanks for all the wonderful works of God.

St Paul reminds us of this in the Letter to the Ephesians:

Sing psalms and hymns and inspired songs among yourselves, singing and chanting to the Lord in your hearts, always and everywhere giving thanks to God who is our Father in the name of our Lord Jesus Christ.

Ephesians 5:15-20

Responsorial Psalm   *Ps 150:1-6*

R   LET EVERYTHING THAT LIVES GIVE PRAISE
    TO THE LORD.

1. Praise God in his holy place,
    praise him in the heavenly vault of his power,
    Praise him for his mighty deeds,
    praise him for all his greatness. R

2. Praise him with fanfare of trumpet,
    praise him with harp and lyre
    praise him with tambourines and dancing,
    praise him with strings and pipes. R

3. Praise him with the clamour of cymbals,
    praise him with triumphant cymbals.
    Let everything that breathes
    praise Yahweh. Alleluia! R

St Luke tells us:

Just at this time, filled with joy by the Holy Spirit, Jesus said, 'I bless you, Father, Lord of heaven and earth, for hiding these things from the learned and the clever and revealing them to little children. Yes, Father, for that is what it has pleased you to do. Everything has been entrusted to me by my Father; and no one knows who the Son is except the Father, and who the Father is except the Son and those to whom the Son chooses to reveal him.'

Luke 10:21-22

Let us pray:

Lord our God, we give you thanks and praise
for all your wonderful works.
We come to dedicate this organ
as an instrument of your praise.
We ask your blessing on it and all who play it.
May it enable us to worship you in spirit and in
    truth.
May it unite us all in harmony of purpose.
May it bring peace to the hearts of all who are
    troubled,
consolation to all in sorrow,
and your joy to all who are weighed down.

We ask your blessing on all who helped to (re)build this organ and on all who made the enterprise possible.

May all who are led to praise you through the music of this organ be joined together for ever in the great hymn of praise that ascends before your throne in heaven. We ask this through Christ our Lord. AMEN.

CIVIC LEADERS

The words of scripture remind us:

Give a shepherd's care to the flock that is entrusted to you; watch over it, not simply as a duty but gladly, as God wants; not for sordid money, but because you are eager to do it. Do not lord it over the group which is in your charge, but be an example for the flock. When the chief shepherd appears, you will be given the unfading crown of glory.

1 Peter 5:2-4

Let us pray:

Lord of all our endeavours,
give to our civic leaders
courage to follow noble aspirations,
strength to support worthy causes,
integrity to seek the truth,
and in all their civic duties,
be their inspiration and guide.

We make this prayer through Christ our Lord.
AMEN.

THOSE WHO WORK IN THE COMMUNICATIONS MEDIA

The human authors Matthew, Mark, Luke and John used their journalistic talents to bring a message of love to millions across the span of nearly two millennia. The 'gospel' message is the good news of our liberation and salvation. It is a message of hope, healing and imagination.

A reading from the Letter to the Romans   *10:14-18*

How then are they to call on him if they have not come to believe in him? And how can they believe in him if they have never heard of him? And how will they hear of him unless there is a preacher for them? And how will there be preachers if they are not sent? As scripture says: How beautiful are the feet of the messenger of good news. But in fact they have not all responded to the good news. Well then, I say, is it possible that they have not heard? Indeed they have: in the entire earth their voice stands out, their message reaches the whole world.

Let us pray:

Eternal God,
we thank you for the gift of writing
and for the modern means of communication.
Help us to use our talents
with honesty, fairness and without prejudice.
May we always seek the truth,
be fearless in exposing corruption,
and have a special concern for those who suffer.
We ask this through Christ our Lord.
AMEN.

62

COMMUNITY LIFE

A reading from the Letter of St Paul to the Romans

12:4-13

Just as each of our bodies has several parts and each part has a separate function, so all of us, in union with Christ, form one body, and as parts of it we belong to each other. Our gifts differ according to the grace given us. If your gift is prophecy, then use it as your faith suggests; if administration, then use it for administration; if teaching, then use it for teaching. Let the preachers deliver sermons, the almsgivers give freely, the officials be diligent, and those who do works of mercy do them cheerfully.

Do not let your love be a pretence, but sincerely prefer good to evil. Love each other, and have a profound respect for each other. Work for the Lord with untiring effort and with great earnestness of spirit. If you have hope, this will make you cheerful. Do not give up if trials come; and keep on praying. If any of the saints are in need you must share with them; and you should make hospitality your special care.

Responsorial Psalm

Ps 133

R   HOW GOOD AND HOW PLEASANT IT IS,
     WHEN PEOPLE LIVE IN UNITY!

1. It is like precious oil upon the head
   running down upon the beard,
   running down upon Aaron's beard,
   upon the collar of his robes. R

2. It is like the dew of Hermon which falls
   on the heights of Zion.

For there the Lord gives his blessing,
life for ever. R

Let us pray:

We ask your blessing, Gracious God, on this
    community.
May it always assemble in peace, in reconciliation,
justice and joy,
in praise of you and service to the world.
May we always accept each other with gratitude
and upbuild each other as members of one body.
Teach us to give instead of demanding,
to trust others rather than compel trust, to serve
    rather than to be served.
Make us thankful for the variety of gifts
and differences of personality that enrich us.
Help us to accept our differences of age,
giving respect to the old and encouragement to the
    young.
Never let us be satisfied with imperfection
but also teach us that patience which is yours.
In peace let us be open to listen
and to speak with readiness to learn.
Purge from our hearts all bitterness, jealousy, and
    thoughts of revenge:
lift us out of depression and sadness.
Let us accept joyfully the service of those who lead
    us, so that we may grow together in love.
May we be one as your Son, Jesus Christ, prayed
    we might be.
With him in the unity of the Holy Spirit
we give you all honour and glory.
AMEN.

A COMPUTER CENTER

We read in the Book of Sirach:

I shall remind you of the works of the Lord,
and tell of what I have seen.
By the words of the Lord his works come into being
and all creation obeys his will.
He has fathomed both the abyss and the human
      heart
and seen into their devious ways;
for the Most High knows all there is to know
and sees the signs of the times.
He declares what is past and what will be,
and reveals the trend of hidden things.
Not a thought escapes him,
not a single word is hidden from him.
He has embellished the magnificent works of his
      wisdom,
he is from everlasting to everlasting,
nothing can be added to him, nothing taken away,
he needs no one's advice.
How lovely, all his works,
how dazzling to the eye!
They all live and last for ever,
and, whatever the circumstances, all obey.
All things go in pairs, by opposites,
he has not made anything imperfect:
one thing complements the excellence of another.
Who could ever grow tired of gazing at this glory?

Ecclesiasticus 42:15.18-25

R   THEIR WORD GOES FORTH THROUGH ALL THE EARTH

1.   The heavens proclaim the glory of God
     and the firmament shows forth the work of his
          hands.
     Day unto day takes up the story
     and night unto night makes known
     the message. R

2.   No speech, no word, no voice is heard
     yet their span extends through all the earth,
     their words to the utmost bounds of
     the world. R

Let us pray:

Lord God, Eternal Wisdom,
look with favour upon the work of our human hands
          and minds.
Guard and protect from all dangers
this computer center,
and all who work in it.
Fill those who give their training and talents in the
          work here
with your Spirit of wisdom and understanding,
of knowledge and good counsel.
May they use these instruments
for the advancement of knowledge and true wisdom,
for the peace and tranquillity of our world.

May almighty God bless you all,
the Father, and the Son, ✠ and the Holy Spirit.
AMEN.

A RECENT CONVERT
TO THE CHURCH

Let us listen to the words of encouragement of the
prophet Isaiah.

The Lord God says this:
You, Israel, my servant,
Jacob whom I have chosen,
descendant of Abraham my friend,
whom I have taken to myself, from the remotest parts
of the earth and summoned from countries far away,
to whom I have said, 'You are my servant,
I have chosen you, I have not rejected you',
do not be afraid, for I am with you;
do not be alarmed, for I am your God.
I give you strength, truly I help you,
truly I hold you firm with my saving right hand.
For I, the Lord, your God,
I grasp you by your right hand;
I tell you, 'Do not be afraid,
I shall help you.'

Isaiah 41:8-10.13

Responsorial Psalm   *Ps 83:2.3-5.8.11*

R   HOW LOVELY IS YOUR DWELLING PLACE,
    LORD, GOD OF HOSTS!

1. My soul is longing and yearning,
    is yearning for the courts of the Lord.
    my heart and soul ring out their joy
    to God, the living God. R

2. The sparrow herself finds a home
    and the swallow a nest for her brood;

she lays her young by your altars,
Lord of hosts, my king and my God. R

3. They are happy, who dwell in your house,
for ever singing your praise.
They are happy, whose strength is in you,
they walk with ever growing strength. R

4. One day within your courts
is better than a thousand elsewhere.
The threshold of the house of God
I prefer to the dwellings of the wicked. R

Let us pray:

_____

For a woman:

Living God, we rejoice in the growth of your
Church
as you add new members to your family.
Through our rebirth in Baptism
you have given us the freedom of the children of
God.
Your servant N,
who has been signed with the cross and anointed
with the oil of salvation, asks for your blessing.
Pour out on her the fullness of your Holy Spirit
to enlighten her mind and lead her to all truth.
United with your priestly people may she be one in
faith and love.
Grant her the courage to put into action the
Baptism received in faith.
May she come to full maturity in the Body of
Christ,
living in holiness as your witness to the world.
Grant her joy in your service.

May she come at last to share in the fellowship of
   the saints
in your eternal kingdom. AMEN.

For a man:
Lord, we rejoice in the growth of your Church
as you add new members to your family.
Through our rebirth in Baptism
you have given us the freedom of the children of
   God.
Your servant N,
who has been signed with the cross and anointed
   with the oil of salvation, asks for your blessing.
Pour out on him the fullness of your Holy Spirit
to enlighten his mind and lead him to all truth.
United with your priestly people may he be one in
   faith and love.
Grant him the courage to put into action the
   Baptism received in faith.
May he come to full maturity in the Body of Christ,
living in holiness as your witness to the world.
Grant him joy in your service.
May he come at last to share in the fellowship of the
   saints
in your eternal kingdom. AMEN.

May God the Father, who made you his child by
   water and the Spirit, watch over you.
May Jesus Christ, the Way, the Truth and the Life,
   lead you always on the path of truth.
May the Holy Spirit, the Comforter, fill your heart
   with true love.
May almighty God bless you, the Father, and the
   Son, ✹ and the Holy Spirit. AMEN.

IN THE EVENT OF A CRIB DEATH

God in his wisdom knows the span of our days: he
has chosen to call N to himself. In the midst of
our pain and sorrow let us turn to him.

The sudden death of N
has bewildered us:
R   BLESS US AND KEEP US, O LORD.

From you human sadness is never hidden,
you know the burden of our grief.   R

You comfort those who mourn.   R

Your wisdom is beyond human understanding.   R

We search for our peace in your will.   R

Let us pray:

Loving God,
you now hold this little one, N, in your arms
and caress him/her in your kindness.
Soothe the hearts of his/her parents,
and bring peace to their lives.
Enlighten their faith
and give hope to their hearts.
We ask this in the name of your Son,
Jesus Christ, our Lord.
AMEN.

CROPS

Let us praise and bless God who provides the fruitful land. Let us listen to the words of Jesus in the Gospel reminding us of the kingdom of heaven.

In Mark's Gospel we read that:

Jesus said: 'This is what the kingdom of God is like. A man scatters seed on the land. Night and day, while he sleeps, when he is awake, the seed is sprouting and growing; how, he does not know. Of its own accord the land produces first the shoot, then the ear, then the full grain in the ear. And when the crop is ready, at once he starts to reap because the harvest has come.'

Mark 4:26-29

Responsorial Psalm   *Ps 64:10-14*

R   TO YOU OUR PRAISE IS DUE, O GOD.

1. You care for the earth, give it water;
    you fill it with riches.
    Your river in heaven brims over
    to provide its grain. R

2. And thus you provide for the earth;
    you drench its furrows;
    you level it, soften it with showers;
    you bless its growth. R

3. You crown the year with your goodness.
    Abundance flows in your steps;
    in the pastures of the wilderness it flows. R

4. The hills are girded with joy,
   the meadows covered with flocks,
   the valleys are decked with wheat.
   They shout for joy, yes, they sing. R

Let us pray:

a) At seed time

Heavenly Father,
giver of our daily bread,
support of the poor and needy,
bless the work of our hands.
Give fruitfulness to this land,
and growth to the seed.
Grant that the earth may bear fruit in abundance
and all our needs may be fulfilled.
We ask this through Christ our Lord.

or

b) At harvest time

We bless and thank you,
Lord, Creator of all things,
for giving us the fruits of the earth in due season.
Make us always grateful for your gifts;
teach us to be content with what we have;
lead us to be generous to those who are in need.
May your blessing be on all who share in the fruits
       of this harvest;
and may we come to share at the table in your
       kingdom where you live and reign for ever and
       ever. AMEN.

May almighty God bless you all,
the Father, and the Son, ✠ and the Holy Spirit.
AMEN.

BEFORE MAKING IMPORTANT DECISIONS 1

We read in scripture:

Jesus exclaimed, 'I bless you, Father, Lord of heaven and of earth, for hiding these things from the learned and the clever and revealing them to mere children. Yes, Father, for that is what it pleased you to do. Everything has been entrusted to me by my Father; and no one knows the Son except the Father, just as no one knows the Father except the Son and those to whom the Son chooses to reveal him.'

Matthew 11:25-30

Let us pray:

Father of all knowledge,
Guide and inspiration of all that is good and holy.
Be with us at this time of crucial decision, be present in our deliberations, be the focus of our striving, be the fullness of our achievement, and the fulfilment of all our endeavours.
AMEN.

BEFORE MAKING IMPORTANT DECISIONS 2

And Jesus said 'Father, if you are willing, take this cup away from me; nevertheless, let your will be done, not mine.'

Luke 22:42

Let us pray:

Lord Jesus, throughout your life on earth you had to make important decisions. Some of them frightened even you. Yet you humbly submitted to the will of your Father and each decision brought you and all of creation nearer to him. Now we have a big decision to make. We need your wishes and your courage so that we too may make the right choice. Be with us, Lord and guide our heart(s) and mind(s) so that whatever we decide to do will create for us an opportunity to grow closer to you, our Saviour, who with the Father and the Holy Spirit lives and reigns for ever and ever. AMEN.

ONE SUFFERING FROM DEPRESSION

There are times when the Lord hides himself from
us in a storm cloud so that, like Jesus in his passion,
we think he has forgotten us utterly.
The psalmist prayed in such isolation:

My soul is thirsting for God,
the God of my life.
My tears have become my bread,
by night, by day.
I will say to God, my rock,
'Why have you forgotten me?
Why do I go mourning,
oppressed by the foe?'

Psalm 41:3.4.10

Let us pray:

Good and gracious God,
we ask you in your loving kindness
to dispel the clouds of depression that are blinding
N.

Be a refuge and strength,
a helper close at hand in time of distress,
that there may be no fear,
though the earth should rock
and the mountains fall into the sea.

Let it be known, no matter what,
that the Lord of Hosts is ever present as a rock and
fortress.
Speak in the darkness your word of comfort:
'Be still and know that I am God'.

Psalm 45

Help N through this trial,
and may that help be shared with all others
who have the same troubles.
We ask this through Christ our Lord.
AMEN.

N, may almighty God bless you,
the Father, and the Son, ✠ and the Holy Spirit.
AMEN.

EASTER EGGS

With joy we celebrate the resurrection of our Lord
Jesus Christ.

If this blessing takes place outside of the Easter
Mass the following psalm may be sung:

Responsorial Psalm   *Ps 117:1-2.16-17*

R   THIS DAY WAS MADE BY THE LORD;
    WE REJOICE AND ARE GLAD.

1. Give thanks to the Lord for he is good,
   for his love has no end.
   Let the sons of Israel say:
   'His love has no end'. R

2. The Lord's right hand has triumphed;
   his right hand raised me up.
   I shall not die, I shall live
   and recount his deeds. R

Let us bless and thank God for these Easter eggs,
signs of new life and of the breaking open of the
tomb by our Lord Jesus Christ.

Blessed are you, Lord, God of life and growth,
you give us food and nourishment
through the wonders of your creation;
as with joy we take these eggs,
may we share in the new life of our risen Saviour
        Jesus Christ,
who, with you and the Holy Spirit, lives and reigns
        for ever and ever. AMEN.

77

AN ELDERLY PERSON

Each period of life has its blessings and its burdens. At all times we can give thanks to God, and we do so today mindful of the wisdom and the serenity of old age.

The Book of Wisdom tells us that:

Length of days is not what makes age honourable, nor number of years the true measure of life; understanding, this is grey hairs, untarnished life, this is ripe old age.

4:8-9

Responsorial Psalm *Ps 125*

R WHAT MARVELS THE LORD WORKED FOR US!
   INDEED, WE WERE GLAD.

1. When the Lord delivered Sion from bondage,
   it seemed like a dream.
   Then was our mouth filled with laughter,
   on our lips there were songs. R

2. The heathens themselves said: 'what marvels
   the Lord worked for them!'
   What marvels the Lord worked for us!
   Indeed we were glad. R

3. Deliver us, O Lord, from our bondage
   as streams in dry land.
   Those who are sowing in tears
   will sing when they reap. R

4. They go out, they go out, full of tears,
   carrying seed for the sowing;

they come back, they come back, full of song,
carrying their sheaves. R

Let us pray:

For a woman:

Eternal God,
we thank you for the long life of N.
May your continual blessing be upon her
and your peace in her heart.
Grant her cheerfulness in good health
and patience in times of bad.
When she worries about the past
give her trust in your abiding mercy:
and when she fears for the future
grant her trust and hope.
Let courage and wisdom guide her daily.
May her family, friends and neighbours
be blessed in their support of her.
May the risen Lord Jesus be her companion on the
     way;
and stay with her when it is towards evening and
     the day is far spent.
May almighty God bless you,
the Father, and the Son, ✳ and the Holy Spirit.
AMEN.

For a man:

Eternal God,
we thank you for the long life of N.
May your continual blessing be upon him
and your peace in his heart.
Grant him cheerfulness in good health

and patience in times of bad.
When he worries about the past
give him trust in your abiding mercy:
and when he fears for the future
grant him trust and hope.
Let courage and wisdom guide him daily.
May his family, friends and neighbours
be blessed in their support of him.
May the risen Lord Jesus be his companion on the
way;
and stay with him when it is towards evening and
the day is far spent.
May almighty God bless you,
the Father, and the Son, ✠ and the Holy Spirit.
AMEN.

AN EMIGRANT

We read in Scripture:

The angel said: 'I shall complete the journey with him. Do not be afraid. On the journey outward all will be well; on the journey back all will be well; the road is safe.' Tobit said, 'Blessings on you, brother!' Then he turned to his son, 'My child', he said 'prepare what you need for the journey, and set off with your brother. May God in heaven protect you abroad and bring you both back to me safe and sound! May his angel go with you and protect you, my child!' Tobias left the house to set out and kissed his father and mother. Tobit said, 'A happy journey!'

Tobit 5:17-22

Let us pray:

For a woman:

Heavenly Father,
we commend to your safe keeping our dear friend
  N,
who departs to another country.
keep her safe on the journey,
give her peace in her heart,
and preserve her from all dangers.
Protect, guide and strengthen her
in her new way of life,
and never let her be separated from you.
We ask this through Christ our Lord. AMEN.

For a man:

Heavenly Father,
we commend to your safe keeping our dear friend
N,
who departs to another country.
Keep him safe on the journey,
give him peace in his heart,
and preserve him from all dangers.
Protect, guide and strengthen him
in his new way of life,
and never let him be separated from you.
We ask this through Christ our Lord. AMEN.

BLESSING

Go forth into the world in peace;
be of good courage;
hold fast that which is good;
render to no one evil from evil;
strengthen the faint-hearted;
support the weak;
help the afflicted;
give honour to all;
love and serve the Lord,
rejoicing in the power of the Holy Spirit.
and the blessing of almighty God, ✠
the Father, and the Son, and the Holy Spirit,
be upon you, and remain with you always.
AMEN.

AN ENGAGED COUPLE

With the Psalmist we pray:

Our soul is waiting for the Lord
The Lord is our hope and our shield
In him do our hearts find joy
We trust in his holy name.

May your love be upon us, O Lord,
as we place all our hope in you.

Let us pray:

Lord our God,
pour out your blessings on N and N. In your
providence you have brought them together. Help
them to prepare well for their marriage. Bring them
closer to each other in respect and trust. As you
have given them to each other, help them to give
themselves to you. May your love be upon them as
they place all their hope in you.
We ask this through Christ, our Lord.
AMEN.

STUDENTS TAKING
EXAMINATIONS

In St Luke's Gospel we read:

Three days later, they found him in the Temple,
sitting among the teachers, listening to them, and
asking them questions; and all those who heard him
were astounded at his intelligence and his replies.

Luke 2:46-48

Let us pray for all students undergoing
examinations:

Lord, pour out your Spirit of Wisdom on these
        students:
help them to remain calm,
to attend carefully to the questions asked,
to think clearly, to remember accurately,
and to express themselves well.

Grant that they may reflect the best of the work
        they have done
and the best of the teaching they have received.
Accept their best efforts in these examinations
and in the great test of life on earth.
May your love be upon them, O Lord,
as they place all their trust in you.

We ask this through Christ our Lord.
AMEN.

THE FAMILY

We read in the Gospel:

He went down with them then and came to Nazareth and lived under their authority. His mother stored up all these things in her heart. And Jesus increased in wisdom, in stature and in favour with God's people.

Luke 2:51-52

Our Lord Jesus Christ gave us the model of family life. He went down with Mary and Joseph and came to Nazareth, and was obedient to them; and his mother kept all these things in her heart. And Jesus increased in wisdom and in stature, and in favour with God and man. Let us pray for God's blessing on this family.

Blessed are you, Lord our God, giver of life:
give your strength and wisdom to the father of this
     family.
Blessed are you, Holy Spirit, bearer of love:
give your compassion and understanding to the
     mother of this family.
Blessed are you, Son of God, eternal wisdom:
give your knowledge and truth to the children of
     this family.
(Blessed are you, Holy Trinity, eternal and
     almighty:
shadow with your protecting wings the
     absent/departed members of this family.)

Let us pray:

Father,
we want to live as Jesus, Mary and Joseph,

in peace with you and with one another.
By following their example in mutual love and
respect
may we come to the joy of our home in heaven.
We ask this through Christ our Lord.
AMEN.

May the Lord bless you and keep you.
May his face shine upon you and be gracious to
you.
May he look upon you with kindness, and give you
his peace.
May almighty God bless you, the Father and the
Son, ✠ and the Holy Spirit. AMEN.

FARM EQUIPMENT

Let us thank God for the gift of the land.

Let the peoples praise you, O God;
let all the peoples praise you.
The earth has yielded its fruit
for God, our God, has blessed us.
May God still give us his blessing
till the ends of the earth revere him.
Let the peoples praise you, O God;
let all the peoples praise you.

Psalm 66:6-8

Let us pray:

We thank you, Creator of all,
that you have established work for our hands,
that we have a project to work upon,
and the tools with which to do the job.
Help us to be appreciative
of all the vehicles, machinery and aids
that technology has produced for our use.
May we use all only in accordance with your desires.
We ask this through Christ our Lord. AMEN.

Let us ask for God's blessing on this equipment
and on all who use it.
Bless, Lord, this equipment, ✳
designed to reap the harvest of riches
provided by you in the world.
May all who use it be kept safe from all danger
and may they thank you always
for the aid it provides in fulfilling your plan
to cultivate and subdue the land.
And may almighty God bless you all,
the Father, and the Son, ✳ and the Holy Spirit.
AMEN.

FATHERS AND MOTHERS

And a voice came from heaven: 'You are my son, whom I love; with you I am well pleased.'

Let us pray:

Dear Lord, we who are fathers and mothers need your help.

You have placed in us the care of each other and of our children.

Give us the strength and patience to cope with the many ups and downs of family life.

Grant us the grace to be deeply thankful for its many laughs, joys and blessings.

Let our children come to know of your love through our love for them.

Help us as we try to make ours a home where love dwells, a home like that of Jesus, Mary and Joseph in Nazareth.

When we fail each other and when we hurt each other, soften our hearts so that forgiveness and reconciliation comes quickly and easily.

Protect this family, Lord, and let it flourish in your light and in your love. We ask this through Christ our Lord. AMEN.

FOR FINE WEATHER

Let us praise God, the creator,
in the words of the Psalmist:

High above, he pitched a tent for the sun,
who comes forth from his pavilion like a
      bridegroom,
delights like a champion in the course to be run.
Rising on the one horizon
he runs his circuit to the other,
and nothing can escape his heat.   *Psalm 19:5-6*

Let us pray:

All powerful and ever living God,
we find security in your forgiveness;
give us the fine weather we pray for
so that we may rejoice in your gifts of
      kindness
and use them always for your
      glory and our good.
We ask this through our Lord Jesus Christ,
your Son, who lives and reigns with you
and the Holy Spirit, one God, for ever and ever.
AMEN.

FOR PROTECTION AGAINST FIRE

In the Book of Daniel we read of God protecting the three young men who had been cast into the furnace of fire. Their prayer for deliverance is expressed in this reading:

We read in the Book of Daniel   *3:25.34-43*

Azariah stood in the heart of the fire, and he began to pray:

Oh! Do not abandon us for ever,
for the sake of your name;
do not repudiate your convenant,
do not withdraw your favour from us,
for the sake of Abraham, your friend,
of Isaac your servant,
and of Israel your holy one,
to whom you promised descendants as countless as
      the stars of heaven
and as the grains of sand on the seashore.
Lord, now we are the least of all nations,
now we are despised throughout the world, today,
      because of our sins.
We have at this time no leader, no prophet, no
      prince,
no holocaust, no sacrifice, no oblation, no incense,
no place where we can offer you the first-fruits
and win your favour.
But may the contrite soul, the humbled spirit be as
      acceptable to you
as holocausts of rams and bullocks,
as thousands of fattened lambs:
such let our sacrifice be to you today,
and may it be your will that we follow you
      wholeheartedly,

since those who put their trust in you will not be
    disappointed.
And now we put our whole heart into following you,
into fearing you and seeking your face once more.
Do not disappoint us;
treat us gently, as you yourself are gentle
and very merciful.
Grant us deliverance worthy of your wonderful
    deeds,
let your name win glory, Lord.

Responsorial Psalm   Ps 123

R   HAVE MERCY ON US, LORD, HAVE MERCY.

1.   To you have I lifted up my eyes,
     you who dwell in the heavens:
     my eyes, like the eyes of slaves
     on the hands of their lords. R

2.   Like the eyes of a servant
     on the hand of her mistress,
     so our eyes are on the Lord our God
     till he show us his mercy. R

We read in the holy Gospel according to Mark:

With the coming of evening, Jesus said to his disciples,
'Let us cross over to the other side'. And leaving the
crowd behind they took him, just as he was, in the boat;
and there were other boats with him. Then it began to
blow a gale and the waves were breaking into the boat
so that it was almost swamped. But he was in the stern,
his head on the cushion, asleep. They woke him and said
to him, 'Master, do you not care? We are going down!'
And he woke up and rebuked the wind and said to the
sea, 'Quiet now! Be calm!' And the wind dropped, and
all was calm again. Then he said to them, 'Why are you

so frightened? How is it that you have no faith?' They were filled with awe and said to one another, 'Who can this be? Even the wind and the sea obey him.'

Mark 4:35:41

Let us pray:

Loving God,
our strength in adversity,
show us at all times your mercy.
Protect our home and all who dwell in it,
especially from the danger of fire.
Do not visit us with the punishments our sins
    deserve
but take away your anger
through the merits of the saving death of your Son,
who lives and reigns with you for ever. AMEN.

Father, give to us and to all your people,
in times of anxiety, serenity;
in times of hardship, courage;
in times of uncertainty, patience;
and at all times a quiet trust in your wisdom and
    love,
through Jesus Christ our Lord. AMEN.

We turn to you for protection,
holy Mother of God.
Listen to our prayers
and help us in our needs.
Save us from every danger,
glorious and Blessed Virgin.

May almighty and merciful God bless and protect
    us,✠
the Father, and the Son, and the Holy Spirit. AMEN.

A GAMBLER

Gambling was a favourite pastime of Roman soldiers.
When the soldiers had crucified Jesus
they divided his garments.
Of his seamless tunic they said,
'Instead of tearing it, let's throw dice to decide who is
to have it.'

John 19:24

Let us pray:

Lord Jesus,
when we first sinned
God ordained that we should eat
bread by the sweat of our brows.
He also ordained that we should be wise
stewards of our material resources in
caring for ourselves and our families.
When you redeemed us
you prayed for those who put you to death
as they threw dice for your tunic.
Help all gamblers to understand God's plan for us.
Help them to use their financial and material resources
wisely, instead of irresponsibly, for their own good and the
good of their families.

PRAYER FOR A
HANDICAPPED CHILD

We read in scripture:

O Lord, my heart is not proud
nor haughty my eyes.
I have not gone after things too great
nor marvels beyond me.

Truly I have set my soul
in silence and peace.
A weaned child on its mother's breast,
even so is my soul.

Psalm 131:1-2

Let us now make this prayer for N.

We thank you, God, for this little one
and the opportunity to love him/her on this earth.

We thank you for the loved ones
who surround us in our family,
and all those people who help
with the daily tasks of looking after this child of yours.

We thank you, God, for the hidden ways
by which you express your love and care to him/her
and help us to show love and affection to him/her.

We thank you for the joy of his/her being
through which this child of yours enjoys the gift of life.

The beautiful purpose of his/her life
will be unfolded among the saints in heaven

where, with our Mother of Perpetual Help,
he/she will praise you, Most Holy Trinity,
Father, Son and Holy Spirit for ever. AMEN.

ONE HANDICAPPED THROUGH AN ACCIDENT

A reading from the Letter to the Hebrews: *10:35-39*

Be as confident now, then, since the reward is so great. You will need endurance to do God's will and gain what he has promised. Only a little while now, a very little while, and the one who is coming will have come; he will not delay. The righteous man will live by faith, but if he draws back, my soul will take no pleasure in him. You and I are not the sort of people who draw back, and are lost by it; we are the sort who keep faithful until our souls are saved.

Let us pray:

For a man:

Heavenly Father, we pray for N in his suffering.
Through his physical incapacity may he learn that
     he is not alone.
May he experience the care and concern of others,
and have the capacity to understand better the
     sufferings of others.
Grant him a closeness with the humanity of Jesus
     Christ, your Son, who suffered and died for us.
Help us to remember that the physical body withers
     away, and that a new life of the spirit awaits us
     through the resurrection
of Jesus Christ, who lives and reigns with you for
     ever and ever. AMEN.

Let us pray:

Heavenly Father, we pray for N in her sufferings.

Through her physical incapacity may she learn that
     she is not alone.

May she experience the care and concern of others,
and have the capacity to understand better the
     sufferings of others.

Grant her a closeness with the humanity of Jesus
     Christ, your Son,
who suffered and died for us.

Help us to remember that the physical body withers
     away, and that a new life of the spirit awaits us
through the resurrection of Jesus Christ,
who lives and reigns with you for ever and ever.
     AMEN.

Almighty God, whose grace is sufficient for all our
     needs,
and whose power comes to full strength in our
     weakness:
we pray for all who suffer and who never get well,
that sustained in their weakness and released from
     pain,
they may rejoice in the power of Christ resting upon
     them.
We ask this in his name. AMEN.

May the Lord bless you and keep you. AMEN.
May his face shine upon you,
and be gracious to you. AMEN.
May he look upon you with kindness,
and give you his peace. AMEN.
May almighty God bless you,
the Father, and the Son, ✠ and the Holy Spirit.
     AMEN.

HANDS

St Paul writes:

As for brotherly love, there is no need to write to you
about that, since you have yourselves learnt from God
to love one another. However, we do urge you to go on
making even greater progress and to make a point of
living quietly, attending to your own business and
earning your living, just as we told you to, so that you
may earn the respect of outsiders and not be dependent
on anyone. *1 Thessalonians 4:9-12*

Let us pray:

Lord God, creator of the universe,
you sent your Son to be one like us.
He came among us working with his hands
in the daily burden of life.
His hands showed your love for us
as he blessed little children,
touched the sick and healed them,
forgave sinners and raised up the dead.
On the cross his hands were pierced
in the great sign of reconciliation.
After his resurrection he showed his hands to his
        disciples
and broke bread with them in peace.
At his ascension his last act was to raise his hands in
blessing on them.

We pray for your blessing on the hands of these,
        your servants,
dedicated to work in the service of others.
Let their hands be signs of your love and concern
        for all.

Let them never weary in their task of healing,
but bring refreshment and comfort to all who suffer.
Protect them from all harm,
and at the last, let them shine forth
as glorious trophies in the splendour of your
        kingdom.
We ask this through Christ our Lord.
AMEN.

May the love of the Lord Jesus draw you to himself;
may the power of the Lord Jesus strengthen you in
        his service;
may the joy of the Lord Jesus fill your souls;
and the blessing of almighty God, ✠
the Father, and the Son, and the Holy Spirit,
be upon you, and remain with you always.
AMEN.

FOR A HAPPY DEATH

Every one of us, every Christian is a pilgrim, a traveller on a journey. That journey begins with Baptism and ends in eternity. Jesus Christ has made the journey before us. He returns to be with us as we travel and is there at the end of the journey to welcome us.

Let us listen to what God's word tells us of the journey's end.

Then I saw a new heaven and a new earth, for the first heaven and the first earth had passed away and there was no longer any sea. I saw a Holy City, the new Jerusalem coming down out of heaven from God, prepared as a bride dressed for her husband. I heard a loud voice call from the throne. Then, 'Look, here God lives among human beings. He will make his home among them; they will be his people, and he will be their God, God-with-them. He will wipe away all tears from their eyes; there will be no more death, and no more mourning or sadness or pain. The world of the past has gone.' Then the One sitting on the throne spoke, 'Look, I am making the whole of creation new'. *Revelation 21:1-5*

Let us pray:

God our Father, Jesus, your Son, has told us that those who have led truly Christian lives are not alone after death but are in his personal presence. You also promise that they will be re-united with us in the future, fully alive in body and spirit.

We ask you now to keep in your special care those* who are close to death. Help them to understand that they are about to receive the reward of their goodness and love and to experience the fulfilment of every hope, joy, peace and love without limit, in Heaven. Give them the assurance of your presence in their last hours so that they may pass easily and peacefully and confidently from this life to you. We invoke the intercession of St. Joseph, patron of a happy death, for those who are dying.

We also ask you to uphold and console all those who mourn them. Light the darkness and fill the emptiness they feel with your peace and healing love. We ask this through Jesus Christ, our Lord, who lives and reigns with you and the Holy Spirit, one God for ever and ever. AMEN.

> * Note: In the case of an individual close to death, this prayer can simply be changed to the singular, adding the person's name.

May the Lord support us all the day long, till the shades lengthen and the evening comes, the busy world is hushed, the fever of life is over and the work is done. Then in his mercy, may he give us a safe lodging, a holy rest and peace at the last. AMEN. *Cardinal Newman*

HARVEST THANKSGIVING

We read in scripture:

Moses said to the people: 'Yahweh your God is bringing you into a fine country, a land of streams and springs, of waters that well up from the deep in valleys and hills, a land of wheat and barley, of vines, of figs, of pomegranates, a land of olives, of oil, of honey, a land where you will eat bread without stint, where you will want nothing. You will eat and have all you want and you will bless Yahweh your God in the rich land he has given you. Be careful not to forget Yahweh your God, neglecting his commandments, customs, and laws.'

Deuteronomy 8:7-10

Responsorial Psalm   *Ps 125*

R   WHAT MARVELS THE LORD WORKED FOR US!

1. The heathens themselves said: 'What marvels
    the Lord worked for them!'
    What marvels the Lord worked for us!
    Indeed we were glad   R

2. Deliver us, O Lord, from our bondage
    as streams in dry land.
    Those who are sowing in tears
    will sing when they reap.   R

3. They go out, they go out, full of tears,
    carrying seed for the sowing;
    they come back, they come back, full of song,
    carrying their sheaves.   R

Blessed are you, Lord God,
you created the earth and its fruits
that we should have food and life.
Blessed are you, Lord Jesus Christ,
who came that we might have life
and have it more abundantly.
We rejoice and give thanks
in the midst of your bounty to us.
May your blessing rest upon
the crops we have saved
to feed both man and beast.
Let us share your blessings
with rich and poor alike.

Let us pray:

Lord God, you are the source of growth and
    abundance.
You have made your creation and our work fruitful
by giving us a rich harvest.
May we gratefully receive the gifts of the earth,
use them wisely and share them unselfishly,
mindful of all who are in need.
We make this prayer through Christ our Lord.

And may the blessing of almighty God,
the Father, and the Son, ✳and the Holy Spirit,
come down upon us and remain with us always.
AMEN.

A HOME

Prepare beforehand: a table and cloth, with an unlit candle, a dish with water; and, if available, a bible, and a crucifix or a picture or statue of the Sacred Heart.

A suitable psalm or hymn could be sung at the beginning and/or the end.

All: **In the name of the Father, and of the Son, and of the Holy Spirit. Amen.**

A member of the household lights the candle, saying:

May the light of Christ shine in this home.

All: **Come and bless the Lord, all you servants of the Lord,**
and all you who serve in the house of the Lord.
Lift up your hands in his holy place,
and bless the Lord always.
May the Lord bless us from his home —
he who made heaven and earth.
Glory be to the Father,
and to the Son,
and to the Holy Spirit,
as it was in the beginning, is now,
and ever shall be, world without end.

Psalm 134

AMEN.

The priest now blesses water to be used in the blessing:

Priest: Lord God almighty,
creator of all life,
of body and soul,
we ask you to bless ✠ this water.
As we use it in faith, forgive our sins.
Lord, in your mercy, give us living water,
always springing up as a fountain of
salvation:
free us, body and soul from every danger,
and admit us into your presence in purity
of heart.
Grant this through Christ, our Lord.

All: AMEN.

If a bible is to be dedicated:

Priest: Let us pray.
Lord Jesus Christ, you are the living
Word of God.
You have the words of everlasting life.
Bless this book of human words, which,
by the gift of your Spirit,
becomes the Word of God.
Through its pages, teach us to know you
better and love you more.
May you, the living Word, be our way,
our truth, and our life — you who live
and reign with the Father and the
Holy Spirit, one God, for ever and ever.

All: AMEN.

Here a chosen passage of Scripture may be
read, for example: Luke 19:1-10; 2
Corinthians 5:6-10; Colossians 3:12-17;
Philippians 4:4-9.

105

LITANY OF BLESSING (adapted from an old Irish blessing).

The lines could be alternated between various persons present, or they could be read by one person.

MAY GOD BLESS THIS HOUSE.

May the Holy Spirit bless this house.

MAY THE HOLY TRINITY BLESS THIS HOUSE.

May Mary bless this house.

MAY ARCHANGEL MICHAEL BLESS THIS HOUSE.

May the holy apostles and martyrs bless this house.

BOTH MORTAR AND CONSTRUCTION.

Both stone and timber.

BOTH CREST AND FRAME.

Both top and foundation

BOTH WINDOW AND WOODWORK.

Both floor and roof.

BOTH HUSBAND AND WIFE.

(Both parents and children.)

BOTH YOUNG AND OLD.

May the King of the elements preserve it.

MAY THE KING OF GLORY TAKE CHARGE OF IT.

May Christ, the gentle son of Mary, pour out the graces of his Holy Spirit on it.

All: AMEN.

ALTERNATIVE PRAYER OF BLESSING
May be read as above.

May God bless this house from its foundation to its roof.

May he bless every doorpost, every stone
and timber.
May he bless the family and the table on
which the food is set.
May he bless every room for sound sleep
at night.
May be bless the door that we open
willingly to the poor and the
stranger, as well as to our relatives.
May he bless the windows which let in the
light to us from sun, moon and stars.
May he bless the roof above our heads,
and each firm wall surrounding us
today.
With our neighbours, may peace and love
abound.
May God bless this family of ours and
keep it from danger; and may he
lead us all to his own kingly house of
hospitality for ever.

All: AMEN.

Each person present may now sign themselves
with the holy water and the sign of the cross,
and water may be sprinkled in the principal
rooms.

If a picture or statue of the Sacred Heart, or a crucifix,
is to be blessed:

Priest: Let us pray.
Almighty God, in your mercy,
bless and make holy this image in honour
of your Son.
Whenever we see it, may we remember

his love and his life for us, and learn to live in him. Grant that whoever prays to and honours your son may receive your grace through him, and give you glory for ever and ever.

All: AMEN.

If the family wishes to dedicate itself to the Sacred Heart of Jesus, the following prayer could be led by a member of the household, or by all together, or by a priest:

Lord Jesus Christ, we gather together today in your name. You promised to be with us all days. We praise and thank you for all your goodness. You are in glory at the right hand of your Father, and you never cease to intercede for us. All our gifts are yours. We thank you for them all, especially for our love of one another as brothers and sisters in your family; and for this home; and for the peace which only you can give. We wish in return to offer our lives to you. Be with us always as the life and centre of this home.

You offered your life for us, and you give yourself to us in the Eucharist. United with you in Baptism, we wish to live by your life. We offer ourselves with you to the Father, and we receive you in Holy Communion. Through your Holy Spirit, strengthen the ties which hold us, and keep us close to you in all we do.

Watch over those who live here; keep them from evil and harm. Guide and bless all they do. Help them to turn to you in prayer. Make their joys holy, and comfort them in their sufferings. In times of trial and sorrow, help them to draw courage and hope from your cross and resurrection.

If ever we sin, grant us the grace to return to you in prayer and penance. Never let anger, resentment or bitterness take hold of us. Keep us one in love and make our hearts like yours — always open to others and ready to forgive.

Give us courage to face the change and partings of life. When death touches us, make us calm and strong in hope, and a comfort to one another. In that hour, be very close to us. Trusting in your love, may we learn to look forward in joyful hope to being united in you forever.

All: AMEN.

Priest: We pray now to the Father with
         confidence as Jesus taught us:

All: Our Father....

Priest: May the blessing of almighty God,
         the Father, the Son, ✠ and the Holy Spirit
         come upon you and your home
         and remain with you for ever.

All: AMEN.

THE HOMELESS

The Lord Jesus was born to a homeless family. St Luke says:

'She gave birth to a son, her first-born. She wrapped him in swaddling clothes and laid him in a manger because there was no room for them in the living space'.

Luke 2:7

or

Jesus was the homeless leader of a band of wandering preachers. He said:

'Foxes have holes and birds of the air have nests, but the Son of Man has nowhere to lay his head'. *Matthew 8:20*

Let us pray:

Lord God, your Son, Jesus Christ, knew the isolation and pain of being homeless. He walked the dusty roads of Galilee without possessions. Many times he slept 'rough' and depended on others for all his needs. We ask your special blessing on all who are homeless or unwanted. Keep close to them and give them the comfort of knowing that you love them. Inspire those in public office to work more strenuously to provide adequate housing and accommodation for all.

Move all Christians to realise that the homeless are Jesus, your Son, asking for help. Make us realise our responsibility to welcome, to help and to integrate into our families and community those who are outcasts and without homes.

Help the homeless to continue to be a reminder to us of some basic values: simplicity of life; the joy of sharing;

110

solidarity with each other and unwavering trust in you as their loving God and Father.

May the Lord bless them and keep them. May he make his face shine upon them and be gracious to them. May he lift up his countenance and give them his peace forever. AMEN.

ONE ILL IN HOSPITAL

Let us read the words of the Apostle Paul:

It makes me happy to be suffering for you now,
and in my own body to make up all the
hardships that still have to be
undergone by Christ for the sake
of his body, the Church.   *Colossians 1:24*

Let us pray:

All-powerful and ever-living God,
the lasting health of all who believe in you
hear us as we ask your loving help for the sick;
restore their health,
that they may again offer joyful thanks in
your Church.
We ask this through Christ, our Lord
AMEN.

THE HOUSEBOUND

We read in the Gospel according to Matthew:

Going into Peter's house
Jesus found Peter's mother-in-law in bed and feverish.
He touched her hand and the fever left her,
and she got up and began to serve him. *Matthew 8:14-15*

Let us pray:

All praise and glory are yours, Lord our God,
for you have called us to serve you in love.
Bless all who have grown old (or weak) in your
    service
and give N strength and courage
to continue to follow Jesus, your Son.
We ask this through Christ our Lord.
AMEN.

INFANT ABNORMALITY

Parents may well ask, in their initial anguish at the birth of an abnormal baby, 'Why has this happened to us?' We are face to face with the mystery of suffering in this situation. Parents need to be comforted, to be assured that it is right and normal to mourn the child they did not have, and then to be helped to accept the child they have been sent.

We read in St John's Gospel:

As Jesus went along he saw a man who had been
blind from birth.
His disciples asked him,
'Rabbi, who sinned, this man or his parents,
that he should have been born blind?'
'Neither he nor his parents sinned,' Jesus said,
'he was born blind so that the words of God might
be revealed in him.'
John 9:1-3

Let us pray:

Gracious God, we believe that this fragile little one
    is sent by you, and for a good purpose;
your works, O God, will be displayed in him/her.
Enable this family to see that they have a baby,
a precious child needing all their love and affection
— a child like any other but who happens to have a
    handicap.
In your compassion, Lord, hear our prayer.

Eternal God, draw the whole family more closely
    together.
Help them to grow strong in supporting one another
and to experience deep joy in the unselfish devotion

which this new member calls forth.
In your compassion, Lord, hear our prayer.

Grant that a caring community will be a source of
strength and support to this family.
In your compassion, Lord, hear our prayer.
And may almighty God,
the Father, the Son and the Holy Spirit,
✠ bless this special child
and all those who welcome and cherish him/her
with a well-spring of joy and peace beyond telling.
AMEN.

FOR INNER HEALING

Jesus said:

'Come to me all you who labour and are
     overburdened,
and I will give you rest.
Shoulder my yoke and learn from me
for I am gentle and humble in heart
and you will find rest for your souls.
Yes, my yoke is easy and my burden light.'

Matthew 11:28-30

Let us pray:

Lord Jesus Christ,
your power reaches to the hidden and unseen
areas of our being.
Touch the mind and heart of our brother/sister, N.
Fill him/her with the strength of your Holy Spirit.
Free him from anxiety, guilt and distress.
Enable him/her to turn to you in faith and love
and to receive your peace and joy,
for you are Lord for ever and ever.
AMEN.

or

Lord Jesus Christ, Redeemer of the world,
you have shouldered the burden of our weakness
and borne our sufferings in your own passion and
     death.
Hear this prayer for our sick brother/sister, N,
whom you have redeemed.
Strengthen his/her hope of salvation.
and sustain him/her in body and soul,
for you live and reign for ever and ever.
AMEN.

A JESSE TREE

We ask God's blessing on our Jesse tree, reminding us of our ancestors before Christ, the Son of David.

We read in sacred scripture:

'A shoot will spring from the stock of Jesse, a new shoot will grow. On him will rest the spirit of Yahweh'.

Isaiah 11:1-2

Let us pray:

Heavenly Father, bless this tree, a reminder to us of your covenanted love, shown to your people, our ancestors, through the events of history in ancient times. May your son Christ, the shoot of Jesse, the true vine, invigorate us with his life and love, so that we may become his living branches in our world today. AMEN.

BEFORE A JOURNEY/PILGRIMAGE

Order of blessing: 1. Introduction
2. Scripture reading
3. Intercessions
4. Blessing

1. Introduction

In the name of the Father, and of the Son, and of
the Holy Spirit. AMEN.
O God, come to our aid.
O Lord, make haste to help us.
Our help is in the name of the Lord,
who made heaven and earth.

2. Scripture reading

As we set out on our journey/pilgrimage let us ask
God's blessing on all we do.

Scripture readings *at choice:*

a) We remember that we are God's pilgrim people and
how his presence goes with us as in the days of his
people's Exodus from Egypt. As he said to the prophet
Isaiah:

And now, thus says Yahweh,
he who created you, Jacob,
who formed you, Israel:
'Do not be afraid, for I have redeemed you;
I have called you by your name, you are mine.
When you pass through the waters I shall be with
you;
or through the rivers, they will not swallow you up.
Should you walk through fire, you will not suffer,
and the flame will not burn you.

118

For I am Yahweh, your God,
the Holy One of Israel, your Saviour'.   *Isaiah 43:1-3*

b) To those whom he calls he gives strength and support,
as we see in the call of Elijah:

But the Angel of Yahweh touched Elijah, and said, 'Get
up and eat, or the journey will be too long for you.' So
he got up and ate and drank, and strengthened by that
food he walked for forty days and forty nights until he
reached Horeb, God's mountain.   *1 Kings 19:7-8*

c) All our journeyings remind us of the final journey
when we go to join our Lord, Jesus Christ, who has gone
before us to prepare a place for us. He said to Thomas:

'I am the Way; I am Truth and Life.
No one can come to the Father except through me.'
    John 14:6

d) From Psalm 138 (*vv 1-3.7-10.3-24*)
O Lord, you search me and you know me,
you know my resting and my rising,
you discern my purpose from afar.
You mark when I walk or lie down,
all my ways lie open to you.

O where can I go from your spirit,
or where can I flee from your face?
If I climb the heavens, you are there.
If I lie in the grave, you are there.

If I take the wings of the dawn
and dwell at the sea's furthest end,
even there your hand would lead me,
your right hand would hold me fast.

O search me, God, and know my heart.
O test me and know my thoughts.
See that I follow not the wrong path
and lead me in the path of life eternal.

e) Psalm 120

I lift up my eyes to the mountains:
from where shall come my help?
My help shall come from the Lord
who made heaven and earth.

May he never allow you to stumble!
Let him sleep not, your guard.
No, he sleeps not nor slumbers,
Israel's guard.

The Lord is your guard and your shade;
at your right side he stands.
By day the sun shall not smite you
nor the moon in the night.

The Lord will guard you from evil,
he will guard your soul.
The Lord will guard your going and coming
both now and for ever.

3. Intercessions

We thank you, Lord, for your goodness to us; for the
health and strength that enables us to travel.
R   BLESSED BE GOD FOR EVER!

We thank you, Lord, for the opportunity given to us
to see the beauty of your creation and to care for it.
R   BLESSED BE GOD FOR EVER!

We thank you, Lord, for friends and company, help us
to grow in love and unity.
R   BLESSED BE GOD FOR EVER!

We thank you, Lord, for the means of travel; help us to go with care and safety.
R   BLESSED BE GOD FOR EVER!

We thank you, Lord, for the blessings of peace and forgiveness: forgive us our sins and offences this day.
R   BLESSED BE GOD FOR EVER!

Let us pray:

Lord, be with us as we travel, and bring us back safely to the place where we long to be: we ask this through Christ our Lord.
AMEN.

Let us ask for the prayers of the saints:

We turn to you for protection,
holy Mother of God.
Listen to our prayers
and help us in our needs.
Save us from every danger,
glorious and blessed Virgin.

St Peter, pray for us.
St Paul, pray for us.
St Francis Xavier, pray for us.
Saint N, pray for us.

4.   Blessings
a)
May almighty God keep you from all harm
and bless you with every good gift.
R   AMEN.

May you walk in the ways of the Lord,
always knowing what is right and good.
R   AMEN.

May your steps be directed to the Lord,
until you enter your heavenly inheritance.
R AMEN.

May almighty God bless you,
the Father, and the Son, ✠ and the Holy Spirit.
R AMEN.

or

b)
May the Lord bless us,
protect us from all evil
and bring us to everlasting life.
R AMEN.

LEISURE/RECREATION CENTER

The Lord created the universe and filled it with delights for us, the People of God. We are called to join in the task of creation by building up the Kingdom. This place which we dedicate today will help us to do that, by restoring us in body and in mind, by drawing us together in community, and by instilling in our people qualities of courage, co-operation and cordiality.

READING FROM SCRIPTURE

Proverbs 6:22-31	The play of creation
Philippians 3:8-21	The goal of life
2 Timothy 4:6-8	Christian life as a race
1 Corinthians 10:23-27	Training for life
1 Corinthians 12:12-26	The body and its parts
Psalm 127	Effort and trust in God
Zephaniah 3:14-17	God dances with us

INTERCESSIONS

Blessed are you, Lord our God, who fills with joy the years of our youth, give our people health and strength.

Blessed are you, Lord our God, who delights in the company of humankind, show us how to relate with each other in true solidarity.

Blessed are you, Lord our God, who endowed the human body with beauty and skill, urge us through the Spirit to put our energy to the service of others.

Blessed are you, Lord our God, who encourages us to use our talents, fill with your grace and integrity our leisure and our play.

Blessed are you, Lord our God, who will dance with us on the Day of the Lord, be with our people in their sport and recreation.

Let us pray:

Living God,
may the place we dedicate today build up humanity,
community, and health among our people.
May the competitions, the games, the contests to be
played here encourage emulation and achievement, not
recrimination and bitterness.
May the various events to be scheduled here bring us
together rather than keep us apart.
May we strive for the prize that lasts.
May our leisure and recreation play its part in building
the kingdom of your love and joy.

We ask this through Christ our Lord. AMEN.

COMFORT AND HOPE IN ANY SITUATION OF LONELINESS

St Paul comforts us when he says:

That I may come to know Christ and the power of his resurrection and partake of his sufferings by being moulded to the pattern of his death, striving towards the goal of resurrection from the dead. Not that I have secured it already, not yet reached my goal, but I am still pursuing it in the attempt to take hold of the prize for which Christ Jesus took hold of me. *Philippians 3:10-12*

Let us pray:

Father of consolation,
be present in the emptiness and loss of this present moment.
Fill our void and nurture our weak spirits.
Source of solace and companion of our ways,
be present in our striving
and give us comfort and hope at this moment
and in the hours ahead.
AMEN.

AT THE START OF THE LORD'S DAY

The celebration of the Lord's day starts on Saturday evening. We celebrate the coming of the first day of the week: the day of the creation of light (Genesis 1:1-5); the day of the resurrection of Jesus (Luke 24:1-8); the day of the coming of the Spirit (Acts 2:1-47); the day of the gathering of the Christian community to celebrate the presence of the risen Jesus among the people gathered in his name (Matthew 18:20); in the proclaiming of the word of Scripture (Luke 24:25-32); and in the breaking of the Bread of Life (Luke 24:33-35). At the start of the Saturday evening meal or at another suitable time, one person may light a candle as a sign of all this, while another prays the following, or a similar prayer, aloud:

Let us pray:

Blessed are you, O Lord our God, our Father, King
    of the universe:
You created light in order to scatter
the darkness of the world.
You raised Jesus, the light of the world,
in order to scatter the darkness of our lives.
You fill us with the Spirit of Jesus
so that we may live by his light.
We bless your holy name
as we kindle this light, (light candle here)
one of your many gifts to us.
Rekindle, we pray, the flame of the Holy Spirit
as we praise you for this day of the Lord.

R   COME, LORD JESUS!
       COME, LORD JESUS!
       COME, LORD JESUS!

One of the readings for Sunday Mass, or one of the readings referred to above, could now be read, with a brief sharing of reflections on it or questions about it.

THOSE WHO WORK IN MEDICINE

A reading from the holy Gospel according to Luke
4:40-42

At sunset all those who had friends suffering from diseases of one kind or another brought them to Jesus, and laying his hands on each he cured them. Devils too came out of many people, howling, 'You are the Son of God'. But he rebuked them and would not allow them to speak because they knew he was the Christ.
When daylight came he left the house and made his way to a lonely place.

Let us pray:

God of all consolation,
your Son Jesus went about healing all manner of diseases;
continue his work today
through the hands of those who work for the sick.
Give them knowledge and wisdom,
patience and sympathy;
and make fruitful their ministry.
We ask this through Christ our Lord. AMEN.

Let us pray:

Send your blessing, Lord God,
upon doctors, nurses and all who assist them.
Enable them to make progress against disease and illness,
to ease the sufferings of the afflicted,
and to encourage healthy living.
May the gifts you have given them
be used to restore the ill to health

so that they may again work for your greater glory.
We ask this through Christ our Lord. AMEN.

May almighty God bless you,
the Father, and the Son, ✠ and the Holy Spirit.
AMEN.

MEN

In scripture we read that God formed man out of the dust of the ground, and breathed into his nostrils the breath of life, and man became a living soul.

Let us pray:

Lord God,
you are the Lord and master of life.
It is your creative power moving within us that ultimately sustains us in existence.
Help us to realise that popularity, success, wealth and achievement will all pass away.
Help us, as men, not to be ashamed to acknowledge our weaknesses, to be tender and kind to others and to recognise you as our Lord and master.

We ask this through Christ our Lord.
AMEN.

ONE SUFFERING FROM MENTAL ILLNESS

Jesus Christ, who suffered such severe mental anguish in Gethsemane, is the one above all others who enters deeply into and shares the suffering of those who are distressed in mind and health.

We read in St Mark's Gospel:

And he began to feel terror and anguish.
And he said to them,
'My soul is sorrowful to the point of death.'
He threw himself on the ground and prayed that,
if it were possible, this hour might pass him by.
'Abba! Father!' he said, 'For you everything is
    possible.
Take this cup away from me.
But let it be as you, not I, would have it.'

Mark 14:32-37

Let us pray:

Father, let those who feel overwhelmed by the dark cloud of mental illness, find comfort in believing that you are with them even though they are unable to experience the joy of your presence.
Let them see that their 'breakdown', which strips them of self-confidence, is in reality a 'breakthrough' to a greater confidence in you and to a new joy and certainty of your loving care, which nothing henceforth can ever destroy or take away. We ask this through Christ our Lord. AMEN.

Let us pray for God's blessing:

May your feelings of loneliness and isolation give way as the friendly words and kindly deeds of others invite you into the warmth of human caring and companionship. Lord, hear us.

R   LORD, GRACIOUSLY HEAR US.

May you come to know the true beauty of your very own being, which God has fashioned with so much love. Lord, hear us.

R   LORD, GRACIOUSLY HEAR US.

As you re-learn how to reach out to help others in their need, may you discover the depths of compassion within yourself and may you find new purpose in using your gifts to affirm and build up others. Lord, hear us.

R   LORD, GRACIOUSLY HEAR US.

May almighty God bless you,
the Father, the Son, ✠ and the Holy Spirit,
And may his peace rise in your heart,
like the sun at daybreak.

AMEN.

PARENTS OF A MENTALLY
HANDICAPPED CHILD

Jesus spoke of the simplicity of children when his disciples asked him who is the greatest in the kingdom of heaven. He told them:

'In truth I tell you, unless you change and become like little children you will never enter the kingdom of heaven. And so, the one who makes himself as little as this little child is the greatest in the kingdom of heaven'.

Let us pray:

Lord God, creator of all things,
we pray for the grace to recognise in our child
this special blessing,
and the opportunity to fulfil our parental duties.

We thank you for N,
who reminds us that your kingdom is not of this
　　world,
and who leads us to a life of faith, hope, confidence
　　and charity.

Let your Holy Spirit of Wisdom guide our every
　　action,
so that we may prepare ourselves and our child
to be in truth your temples.

May Mary, who accepted the sword of suffering in
　　her own life,
help us to accept with love all daily burdens.

Grant that we may attach ourselves to you alone.
We offer you each day

our joys and sorrows
that you may render them pleasing in your sight,
so that tomorrow we may not come before you with
    empty hands.
To you be praise and blessing and thanksgiving,
through Jesus Christ our Lord. AMEN.

MILITARY PERSONNEL

A reading from the holy Gospel according to John

14:27

Jesus said to his disciples:
'Peace I bequeath to you,
my own peace I give you,
a peace the world cannot give, this is my gift to
        you.
Do not let your hearts be troubled or afraid.'

Let us pray:

Lord God of hosts,
bless all who serve our country in the cause of peace
on land and sea, and in the air.
Help them and those in authority who lead them to
discern prayerfully whether a potential conflict or war
is just.
Help them to meet all danger with courage;
let them be models of discipline and loyalty.
We ask this through Christ our Lord. AMEN.

(On the occasion of going on overseas duty)
Let us pray for those who are going abroad in the cause
        of peace:
God, you sent your Son Jesus Christ as the Prince
of Peace.
Send your blessings on these soldiers who respond to
        the needs of peacekeeping.
Keep them safe from harm.
Let them be models of discipline and courage,
and bring them home safely to their loved ones.
May they work loyally to build up your kingdom of
        peace, love and justice.
We ask this through Christ our Lord. AMEN.

Go forth into the world in peace;
be of good courage;
hold fast that which is good;
render to no-one evil for evil;
strengthen the faint-hearted;
support the weak;
help the afflicted;
honour all men;
love and serve the Lord,
rejoicing in the power of the Holy Spirit.
And may the blessing of almighty God,
the Father, the Son, ✻ and the Holy Spirit,
be upon you,
and remain with you for ever. AMEN.

LAY MINISTERS

Jesus proclaimed:

The greatest among you must behave as if he were the youngest, the leader as if he were the one who serves. For who is the greater: the one at table or the one who serves? Yet here am I among you as one who serves!

Luke 22:26-27

Let us pray:

Lord of gentleness,
renew the ministers of your Church with food and drink from heaven.

Keep them faithful as ministers of Word and Sacrament, that they might grow in humility, and work for your glory and for the salvation of those who believe in you.

We make this prayer through Christ our Lord, AMEN.

PARENTS WHO HAVE SUFFERED A MISCARRIAGE

Jeremiah tells us:

The word of the Lord came to me saying:
'Before I formed you in the womb I knew you;
before you came to birth I consecrated you'.

Jeremiah 1:1

God has called each of us to himself
Our little one is with you and sees you face to face:
R   BE WITH US LORD.

In you life is changed, not taken away:
R   BE WITH US LORD.

Comfort us in this time of apparent absurdity and
        contradiction:
R   BE WITH US LORD.

Fill the emptiness that gnaws within us:
R   BE WITH US LORD.

(Even in the face of death we praise and thank you
        for the gift of life:
R   BE WITH US LORD.)

Let us pray:

Lord God,
ever caring and gentle,
we commit to your love this little one,
quickened to life for so short a time.
(Lord, you formed this child in the womb;
you have known it by name before time began.

138

We now wish to name this little one N;
a name we shall treasure in our hearts for ever.)

Bless these parents
who are saddened by the loss of their baby.
Give them courage
and help them in their pain and grief.
May they all meet one day
in the joy and peace of your kingdom.

We ask this through Christ our Lord. AMEN.

MISSING PERSONS

We read in the Gospel how, as a child, Jesus was lost in Jerusalem and was found in the Temple. And Mary his mother said to him,
'My child, why have you done this to us? See how worried your father and I have been, looking for you.' He went down with them and came to Nazareth.   *Luke 2:48-51*

Let us pray:

God our Father,
your Son Jesus Christ as a child
was lost in the chaos of a great city
and was restored to the love of his family;
watch over N, now missing, for whom we pray
and protect him/her with your love.
Be near to those who are anxious for him/her;
let your presence change their sorrow into comfort,
their anxiety into trust,
their despair into faith,
that they may know your loving purposes.
And this we ask
in the name of Jesus our Lord,
who loves and lives
and cares for all your children. AMEN.

BLESSING

May Christ draw you to himself
that you may find in his cross
a sure ground for faith
and a firm support for hope:
and the blessing of God almighty,
the Father, the Son, ✶ and the Holy Spirit,
be with you and remain with you always. AMEN.

MISSIONARIES

Jesus said:

'Go, therefore, make disciples of all nations;
baptise them in the name of the Father and
of the Son and of the Holy Spirit.'   *Matthew 28:19*

Let us pray:

God our Father,
Lord of the harvest,
continue to guide and empower
the worldwide mission of the Church,
so that your desire to make disciples
of all nations may become a reality in our day.

Inspire all those engaged in the missions
with zeal, strength, perseverance and hope,
so that, having gone forth to sow the seed
of your Word in every land,
they may rejoice in a rich harvest
of souls for the kingdom of God.

We make our prayer through our Lord Jesus Christ.
AMEN.

BLESSING

For a woman:
We ask you now to bless N,
who leaves us to share in this work of mission.
Protect her on the journey.
Open the hearts of all who meet her

that they may accept her in love.
Guide her with the gifts of the Holy Spirit
that she may be an instrument of your grace.
Give her courage and peace at all times.
We ask this through Christ our Lord.
AMEN.

For a man:

We ask you now to bless N,
who leaves us to share in this work of mission.
Protect him on the journey.
Open the hearts of all who meet him
that they may accept him in love.
guide him with the gifts of the Holy Spirit
that he may be an instrument of your grace.
Give him courage and peace at all times.
We ask this through Christ our Lord.
AMEN.

N, may almighty God bless you, ✠
the Father, and the Son, and the Holy Spirit. AMEN.

A NEW HOME

As N and N move into this house, we gather to ask that peace may come upon them, their new house and all who will live or visit here in the future.

The Lord Jesus said to his disciples:

'Whatever town or village you go into, seek out someone worthy and stay with him until you leave. As you enter his house, salute it, and if the house deserves it, may your peace come upon it.' *Matthew 10:11-12*

We listen to St Paul telling us how Christians should live. It is our prayer today that this vision will always animate and inspire this family:

'Let love be without any pretence. Avoid what is evil; stick to what is good. In brotherly love let your feelings of deep affection for one another come to expression and regard others as more important than yourself. In the service of the Lord, work not half-heartedly but with conscientiousness and an eager spirit. Be joyful in hope, persevere in hardship; keep praying regularly; share with any of God's holy people who are in need; look for opportunities to be hospitable'. *Romans 12:9-16*

(It might be worthwhile to bless some religious object — statue, picture, banner, etc. — at this time).

Let us pray:

God, our Father, today in your name, we bless this new house with water. Water has always been seen as a symbol of refreshment, of growth, of new beginnings and of your ever-present action amongst us. This house marks a new beginning for this family. May it always be a haven of refreshment and peace, a place of new life and growth and a domestic Church where you are respected, worshipped and regularly addressed in prayer. This water is also a reminder of our Baptism. Help us 'to live always as children of the light, keeping the flame of faith alive in our hearts'. May this religious object remind us of our baptismal commitment to your Son, Jesus Christ, who is our Lord for ever and ever. AMEN.

It is suggested that blessings might be pronounced at a few locations in the home. For example:

At the main door

Through this door you will return, weary from the demands and pressures of work or school. May you always be able to relax here in an atmosphere of love, acceptance, understanding and sharing. May you go out from here to spread peace and love among those you meet and help to build up God's kingdom on earth. May this door always offer hospitality to visitors, to strangers and to the needy. May you welcome them as Jesus Christ, seeking your companionship and help.

In the kitchen/living room

In this room, you gather to share food together, to work and to play, to talk and to help each other. May the Lord keep you always united in love. May the children, NN, be encouraged, supported and helped to grow to Christian maturity. May this room also be a place where you turn to God, your ever-loving Father, in daily family prayer, and when life's pilgrimage is over, may this family be re-united in the unending joy and peace and love of our heavenly home.

In one of the bedrooms

The Lord upholds us while we are awake and guards us while we sleep. He helps us to walk in his way of love. We thank you for the goodness N and N recognise in each other, for the love they share and for the generosity and care they give their children.

May your love for each other grow stronger day by day. May your joy be increased by your mutual sharing of it and may your closeness soften whatever adversity you may meet.

Let us now pray together in the words that Jesus gave his closest followers: 'Our Father....'

> (Some gesture of exchanged greeting might be suitable at this point.)

FINAL BLESSING

Let us bow our heads and pray for God's blessing:

May the Father love you and come to you and live with you. AMEN.

May the Son of God stay with you and give you his peace. AMEN.

May the Spirit of God teach you all things and stay with you forever. AMEN.

May the blessing of almighty God, Father, Son, ✠ and Holy Spirit come upon you and remain with you forever. AMEN.

> (Individual phrases/sections of the above which would be inapplicable would be omitted).

NEWLY-WEDS

Blessed be the Lord, the God of Israel;
for he has visited his people, he has set them free.
and he established for us a saving power
in the house of his servant David.
Because of the faithful love of our God
the rising sun has come from on high to visit us,
to give light to those who live
in darkness and the shadow dark as death,
and to guide our feet
into the way of peace.

Luke 1:68,79; The Song of Zechariah

Let us pray:

Blessed are you,
O Lord our God, king of the universe;
we bless you each day of our married life.
Renew your blessing within us
as we choose each day, by your grace,
to be a living sign of your eternal love;
may we come to know, love, accept,
forgive, and encourage each other anew.
We ask you to guide us today, as....
(either or both could mention whatever situation
seems important)
for the kingdom, the power, and the glory are yours
now and for ever.
AMEN.

Scripture for reflection: 1 John 4:7-12; or any of
the Scripture readings suggested for weddings.

BEFORE AN OPERATION

We read in scripture:

My child, when you are ill, do not rebel, but pray to the Lord and he will heal you. Renounce your faults... and cleanse your heart from all sin. Then let the doctor take over — the Lord created him too — and do not let him leave you, for you need him. There are times when good health depends on doctors. For they, in their turn will pray the Lord to grant them the grace to relieve and to heal, and so prolong your life. *Ecclesiasticus 38:9-14*

Let us pray:

Lord God, our lives are in your hands. Be with us now at this crucial moment. Guide the hands and inspire the skill of the doctors and nurses to bring this operation to a successful conclusion, so that N may recover his/her full health speedily to the glory of your name.

We make our prayer through our Lord Jesus Christ. AMEN.

ORPHANS 1

Jesus reminds us:

'That is why I am telling you not to worry about your life and what you are to eat, nor about your body and how you are to clothe it.... Look at the birds in the sky.... the flowers growing in the fields.... Are you not worth more than they are? It is the gentiles who set their hearts on all those things. Your heavenly Father knows that you need them... so do not worry about tomorrow: tomorrow will take care of itself.'   *Matthew 6:25-32*

'There is no need to be afraid; you are worth more than many sparrows'.   *Matthew 10:31*

Let us pray:

Heavenly Father,
you are a God who cares for all of your children.
In your kindness look with special love
on all those who are orphaned
and have been left without parental love and care.

Give these your children peace of mind.
Deliver them from all unnecessary fear and anxiety
about their past, present and future.

Just as you care for the birds of the air,
the flowers of the fields,
help all orphans to know how much more precious
they are in your sight,
how you call each of them by name,
and carry them in the palm of your hand.
AMEN.

ORPHANS 2

Jesus reminds us:

'Let the little children come to me; do not stop them;
for it is to such as these that the kingdom of God belongs.
In truth I tell you, anyone who does not welcome the
kingdom of God like a little child will never enter it.'
Then he put his arms around them, laid his hands on
them and gave them his blessing.   *Mark 10:14-16*

St James tells us that:

Pure, unspoilt religion, in the eyes of God our Father,
is this: coming to the help of orphans and widows when
they need it, and keeping oneself uncontaminated by the
world.   *James 1:27*

Let us pray:

Lord Jesus our brother,
you have revealed to us that God is our loving
          Father.
Bless all children who have been deprived of
parental love and affection;
protect and guide all orphans in their journey
          through life.
May they discover the love you have for them,
through the care and support
they receive from those they meet.
Make them conscious of your nearness to them,
and help them know that they are never alone.
And may Mary, Mother of us all, love the unloved,
the lost and the lonely.
AMEN.

ONE IN PAIN

Jesus has gone before us on the path of suffering. He is our model and support; let us remember his last agony.

We read in John's Gospel:

After this, Jesus knew that everything had now been completed, and so that the scripture should be completely fulfilled he said:
'I am thirsty.'
A jar full of sour wine stood there, so, putting a sponge soaked in the wine on a hyssop stick they held it up to his mouth. After Jesus had taken the wine he said:, 'It is fulfilled.' And bowing his head he gave up his spirit.

John 19:28-30

Let us pray:

Heavenly Father,
your Son bore his agony on the cross for us:
bless N, who now shares that suffering with him.
Strengthen him/her in this hour of need.
Help us to be of service
so that this burden of pain may be eased.

We ask this through Christ our Lord.

And may almighty God bless you,
the Father, and the Son, ✠ and the Holy Spirit.
AMEN.

PARENTS OF A HANDICAPPED CHILD

If the eyes of Jesus had rested on a little handicapped child, this is surely one he would have chosen to set before his disciples. And it is easy to imagine with what extra gentleness and affection Jesus would have held this little one in his arms.

We read in Mark's Gospel:

Jesus took a little child whom he set among them
    and embraced, and he said to them,
'Anyone who welcomes a little child such as this in
    my name, welcomes me;
and anyone who welcomes me, welcomes not me but
    the one who sent me.'
                                  Mark 9:37

Let us pray:

Loving Father, your Son, Jesus, was sensitive to the
    needs of parents who drew close to him with
    their children.
Look with special compassion on the hearts of
    parents who have a handicapped child.
Help them to realise that in welcoming their little
    child they are welcoming Jesus whom you sent.
May this truth fill their hearts with a gladness and
    peace beyond all telling.
In their acceptance of this handicapped child may
    they grow in strength, love and maturity.
May the hearts of this child's parents reverberate
    with the love of your own heart.

May almighty God, Father, Son ✠ and Holy Spirit, touch and bless the hearts of all mothers and fathers. AMEN.

FOR PEACE

Jesus said:

'My own peace I give you; a peace which the world cannot give, this is my gift to you. Do not let your hearts be troubled or afraid.'   *John 14:27*

Let us pray:

Lord God, our Father,
you seek the welfare of your children
and not their destruction:
direct our wills towards the peace for which we
        yearn;
and let there be peace among the nations,
peace in our land,
peace in our homes,
and peace in our hearts;
that we may know that peace
which passes all understanding
in Jesus Christ our Lord. AMEN.

God grant to the living, grace;
to the departed, rest;
to the Church, our country and all humanity,
peace and concord;
and to us and all his servants, life everlasting;
and may almighty God bless us,
the Father, the Son, ✠ and the Holy Spirit. AMEN.

POVERTY SITUATION

We read in the Gospel:

Then he took the five loaves and the two fish,
raised his eyes to heaven and said the blessing;
then he broke the loaves and began handing them
to his disciples to distribute among the people.
He also shared out the two fish among them all.
They all ate as much as they wanted.   *Mark 6:41-42*

Let us pray:

God our Father,
your Son Jesus Christ looked with compassion on
        the hungry and came to their assistance;
hear us,
who pray in his name
for those in poverty and want;
help us,
who have so much,
to live more simply
that others may simply live;
and prosper our efforts for relief and aid
that there may be found
food sufficient for all humanity;
we ask this through Jesus Christ our Lord. AMEN.

May the love of the Father enfold us,
the wisdom of the Son enlighten us,
the fire of the Spirit inflame us;
and may God shower his blessings
on us and all his children
now and for ever more. AMEN.

POVERTY SITUATION IN THE FAMILY 1

We read in the Book of Deuteronomy:

'Is there anyone poor among you, one of your brothers, in any town of yours in the country which Yahweh your God is giving you? Do not harden your heart or close your hand against that poor brother of yours but be open handed with him and lend him enough for his needs... and that is why I am giving you this command: Always be open handed with your brother, and with anyone in your country who is in need and poor'.

Deuteronomy 15:7-11

Let us pray:

Father,
we live in a world where some have too little and others too much.
Your commandment of love is ignored and laughed at.
Help us not to feel bitter but to remember that you love those who suffer in a special way.
Never let us lose hope.
Help us to continue the struggle to ensure that all may have their basic needs met and soften the hearts of those who do not care.
We ask this, with trust in your providence, through your Son, Jesus, who is Lord for ever and ever. AMEN.

POVERTY SITUATION IN THE FAMILY 2

Why, Yahweh, do you keep so distant,
stay hidden in times of trouble?
In his pride the wicked hunts down the weak
who is caught in the schemes he devises.   *Psalm 10:1-2*

Let us pray:

All powerful Father,
God of Mercy,
look kindly on us in our suffering.
Ease our burden and make our faith strong
that we may always have confidence and trust
in your fatherly care.
Grant this through our Lord Jesus Christ,
your Son, who lives and reigns with you for ever
      and ever.

FOR SAFETY IN PREGNANCY

We read in Scripture:

Can a woman forget her baby at the breast,
feel no pity for the child she has borne?   *Isaiah 49:15*

God is like a mother who never forgets her baby, who
always loves the child to whom she gives birth. Knowing
that God is present and active during this pregnancy,
we pray with confidence:

You are the giver of life:
R   KEEP US SAFE IN THE PALM OF YOUR HAND, O GOD.

You entrust this new life to our care;
R   KEEP US SAFE IN THE PALM OF YOUR HAND, O GOD.

You know our worries for the safety of our child:
R   KEEP US SAFE IN THE PALM OF YOUR HAND, O GOD.

As we draw nearer to the time of birth:
R   KEEP US SAFE IN THE PALM OF YOUR HAND, O GOD.

As we wait in joyful hope,
R   KEEP US SAFE IN THE PALM OF YOUR HAND, O GOD.

Let us pray:

God, you formed man and woman in your own image
and likeness and invited them to share with you in the
creation of new life.

Bless this child; keep it safe and free from all harm.
Bless this mother; give her peace of mind and health of

157

body, as she nourishes the new life within her.
(Bless this father; give him strength and understanding to support his wife (this mother) as their child grows within the womb.)

(Bless this couple; may this new life in which they share draw them closer to each other and to you Lord, the creator and giver of life.)

We ask this through Christ our Lord. AMEN.

PRIESTS

We read in Matthew's Gospel:

> Jesus made a tour through all the towns and villages,
> teaching in their synagogues, proclaiming the good news
> of the kingdom and curing all kinds of disease and all
> kinds of illness. And when he saw the crowds he felt sorry
> for them because they were harassed and dejected, like
> sheep without a shepherd. Then he said to his disciples,
> 'The harvest is rich but the labourers are few, so ask the
> Lord of the harvest to send out labourers to his harvest.'
>
> *Matthew 9:35-37*

Let us pray:

Lord Jesus,
you have chosen your priests from among us
and sent them out to proclaim your Word,
to celebrate the Eucharist for the faithful, and
to act in your name.
For so great a gift to your Church,
we give you praise and thanksgiving.

Inspire them through prayer to live each day
the mystery of your dying and rising.
Make them constant in prayer for poor sinners.
May the Holy Spirit put your word on their lips
and your love in their hearts,
to bring good news to the poor
and healing to the broken-hearted.

And may the gift of Mary your mother,
to the disciple whom he loved,
be your gift to every priest.
Grant that she who formed you in her human
    image,

may form them in your divine image,
by the power of your Spirit,
to the glory of God the Father. AMEN.

Let us pray for God's blessing upon these priests*:
   (*The singular version may be used when
      required.)

Heavenly Father,
send your blessing upon these chosen ones.
Fill them with the fire of your love,
that their ministry may reveal your presence in the
   Church.
May your power shine out through their weakness,
since they are earthen vessels.
In their affliction let them never be crushed;
in their doubts never despair;
in temptation never be destroyed;
in persecution never abandoned.
In times of weakness send them your Spirit,
and help them always to praise you
now and forever.
AMEN.

And may the blessing of almighty God,
the Father, and the Son, ✠ and the Holy Spirit,
come down upon us and remain with us for ever.
AMEN.

PRISONERS

We read in St John's Gospel:

Jesus said:
If you make my word your home
you will indeed be my disciples,
you will learn the truth
and the truth will make you free.
I tell you most solemnly,
everyone who commits sin is a slave.
Now the slave's place in the house is not assured,
but the son's place is assured.
So if the Son makes you free,
you will be free indeed.   *John 8:31-36*

Let us pray:

We pray, our Father, for those whose freedom has
    been taken away from them:
for all who suffer imprisonment, whether for crime
    or for the sake of conscience;
for all whose vision of your world is seen through
bars, and in whose heart the lamp of hope burns
    low.
God of mercy, give them help according to their
    need, and hear our prayers for Jesus Christ's
    sake. AMEN.

BLESSING

For a woman:
God of mercy, send your blessing on N.
Give her the courage to put up patiently with
                prison life,

to endure boredom and hardship,
to be tolerant of others,
and allow her to taste freedom through an early
    release.
We ask this through Christ our Lord. AMEN.

For a man:

God of Mercy, send your blessing on N.
Give him the courage to put up patiently with
    prison life,
to endure boredom and hardship,
to be tolerant of others,
and allow him to taste freedom through an early
    release.
We ask this through Christ our Lord. AMEN.

May almighty God bless you,
the Father, and the Son, ✠ and the Holy Spirit.
    AMEN.

FOR RAIN

We read in the Book of Job:

If I were you, I should appeal to God
and lay my case before him.
His works are great, past all reckoning,
marvels beyond all counting.
He sends down rain to the earth,
pours down water on the fields.   *Job 5:8-10*

Let us pray:

Lord God,
in you we live and move and have our being.
Help us in our present time of trouble,
send us the rain we need,
and teach us to seek your lasting help
on the way to eternal life.
We ask this through Christ our Lord. AMEN.

RELIGIOUS ARTICLES
(CRUCIFIXES, STATUES, MEDALS, SCAPULARS ETC., USED IN PRIVATE DEVOTION)

We use these symbols of religious devotion to remind us of God's love for us and the saving work of our Lord Jesus Christ. Let our lives show a spirit of prayer and conformity to God's holy will at all times. Let us listen to the words of Jesus:

St Luke tells us that:

Jesus said: So I say to you: Ask, and it will be given to you; search, and you will find; knock, and the door will be opened to you. For everyone who asks receives; everyone who searches finds; everyone who knocks will have the door opened. *Luke 11:9-10*

Responsorial Psalm *Ps 102*

R   HAVE MERCY ON US, LORD, HAVE MERCY.

1. To you have I lifted up my eyes,
   you who dwell in the heavens;
   my eyes, like the eyes of slaves
   on the hands of their lords. R

2. Like the eyes of a servant
   on the hand of her mistress,
   so our eyes are on the Lord our God
   till he show us his mercy. R

3. Have mercy on us, Lord, have mercy.
   We are filled with contempt.
   Indeed all too full is our soul
   with the scorn of the rich,
   (the disdain of the proud). R

164

Let us pray:

Blessed are you, Lord, God of power and might:
you have called us to worship you in spirit and in
truth;
and have given us signs of your love
in creation and in the work of your Son, Jesus
Christ.
He has called us to pray continually
and to call upon you, Father, in all our needs.

Send your blessing upon these symbols of faith
and upon all who use them devoutly;
that looking upon them
they may be drawn to the vision of your goodness
and conform their lives to the likeness of
Jesus Christ,
who lives and reigns with you for ever and ever.
AMEN.

May almighty God bless you all
the Father, and the Son, ✠ and the Holy Spirit.
AMEN.

THOSE CONTEMPLATING
JOINING RELIGIOUS LIFE

Jesus said:

'The harvest is rich but the labourers are few, so ask the Lord of the harvest to send out labourers to his harvest'.

Matthew 9:37

Let us pray:

Father, in every age you gather a people to yourself and you choose men and women to proclaim the Lordship of Jesus your Son. Bless those among us whom you call to leave all things out of zeal for the Gospel of Christ and love for his holy Church. May the witness of our lives be a light to their path and a source of lasting encouragement.
We ask this, Father,
in the name of Jesus the Lord.
AMEN.

A RELIGIOUS SISTER

In the Gospel according to St John,
Jesus says to his disciples:

'You did not choose me,
no, I chose you;
and I commissioned you
to go out and to bear fruit,
fruit that will last:
and then the Father will give you
anything you ask him in my name.
My command to you
is to love one another.'   *John 15:16-17*

Let us pray for God's blessing:

May almighty God bless you
as you show to the world the immensity of divine
      love;
may Jesus Christ bless you
as you follow him in feeding the multitude who
      hunger in body and soul;
may the Holy Spirit bless you
as you work for peace, unity and love among all
      people.
And may the vows that bind you on earth
lead you to the community of eternal love
in the Holy Trinity for ever and ever.
AMEN.

RELIGIOUS SISTERS AND WOMEN LIVING IN COMMUNITY

Paul, writing to the Christian community in Rome said:

I am certain of this: neither death nor life, nor angels, nor principalities, nothing already in existence and nothing still to come, nor any power, nor the heights, nor the depths, nor any created thing whatever will be able to come between us and the love of God, known to us in Christ Jesus our Lord.   *Romans 8:38-39*

Let us pray for those women who are bound together by the love of God to live a shared life in religious and lay communities.

O God, we ask your blessing on all these women who have chosen to love and serve you with their sisters in Christ in community. May they live in the sure knowledge that nothing can separate them from your love which binds them together as they share the one bread of life. May they reveal the joy and hope which comes from knowing you, the abundant life which your Son came to bring. May they have the courage not only to be fellow pilgrims with all who journey to you but also to take new initiatives under the guidance of the Holy Spirit which will hasten the coming of the kingdom.

We make this prayer in the name of him who made God's love visible, Jesus Christ our Lord. AMEN.

ONE WHO HAS LEFT RELIGIOUS LIFE

The vocation to live the Gospel is given to everyone in the Church; the vocation to religious life is given only to some. In the Gospel Jesus says to one: 'Go, sell all you possess and come follow me', but to another he says: 'go home to your family and tell them how much the Lord in his mercy has done for you'.

Let us pray:

Father of love and mercy,
bless the desire to follow you that is in N.
Reward the generous service already given to your
       people;
and find for him/her
peace in your Church
and that happiness of living according to your
       perfect will.
We ask this through Christ our Lord.
AMEN.

May almighty God bless you,
the Father, and the Son, ✠ and the Holy Spirit.
AMEN.

ROSARY BEADS

The Angel Gabriel was sent by God to seek Mary's agreement to become the mother of his son. Gabriel said, 'Rejoice, you who enjoy God's favour!'   *Luke 1:28*

Jesus taught his disciples to pray the Our Father.

Let us pray:

God our Father,
through Mary you chose
to give the Rosary to St Dominic
for the whole Church.
In the Rosary we contemplate the great truths of faith.
Help us to think on the mysteries in the life of your son in the company of his mother.
Bless these beads. ✤
Grant that by their use
we may give glory to the Father, Son and Holy Spirit.   AMEN.

A SCHOOL EXTENSION/NEW CLASSROOMS ETC.

In St Paul's First Letter to the Corinthians, he says:

We do share in God's work; you are God's farm, God's building. By the grace of God which was given to me, I laid the foundations like a trained master-builder, and someone else is building on them. Now each one must be careful how he does the building. For nobody can lay down any other foundation than the one which is there already, namely Jesus Christ.   *1 Corinthians 3:9-11*

Responsorial Psalm   *Ps 126*

R   THEY BUILD IN VAIN WITHOUT THE LORD.

1. If the Lord does not build the house,
    in vain do its builders labour;
    if the Lord does not watch over the city,
    in vain do the watchers keep vigil. R

2. In vain is your earlier rising,
    your going later to rest,
    you who toil for the bread you eat:
    when he pours gifts on his beloved while they
    slumber. R

3. Yes, children are a gift from the Lord,
    a blessing, the fruit of the womb.
    Indeed the sons of youth
    are like arrows in the hand of a warrior. R

St Mark tells us:

People were bringing little children to him, for him to

touch them. The disciples scolded them, but when Jesus saw this he was indignant and said to them, 'Let the little children come to me; do not stop them; for it is to such as these that the kingdom of God belongs. In truth I tell you, anyone who does not welcome the kingdom of God like a little child will never enter it.' Then he embraced them, laid his hands on them and gave them his blessing.

Mark 10:13-16

Let us pray for God's blessing on this building:

Almighty God, send your blessing upon this building
which has been set apart for the pursuit of learning,
that it may always be a home of truth and wisdom.
Bless all who will work in it,
give encouragement and strength to teachers
as they follow their vocation.
Give to the pupils health and wisdom
and the grace to love you and one another
as Jesus, your Son, loved us.
May they grow in wisdom and grace
and be able to live richly human and Christian lives
in the world that lies before them.
Bless all those who played a part
in the provision of this building:
in its planning, in its design,
in its construction, in its financing.
Bless all of us as we renew our dedication to the truth.
This we ask through Jesus Christ, our Lord.
AMEN.

And may almighty God bless you all,
the Father, and the Son, ✠ and the Holy Spirit.
AMEN.

ON THE OCCASION OF A SCHOOL VISIT

The occasion for this may be at the end of a lesson when scripture will have been already used.

Let us pray for God's blessing on all within this school.

a) Father of us all,
bless the children/pupils/young people of this class
as they prepare for their vocations in life.
Let them always be thankful for the gifts of mind
you have given them, may they use their opportunities
to develop all their talents, and learn strength of spirit
to serve each other through life.
We ask this through Christ our Lord. Amen.

b) Loving Lord,
bless the children/pupils/young people of this class
that they may gain faith and knowledge for the journey
of life.
May they learn each day to gain the self-discipline
that will help them control their lives:
may they grow in integrity of character
learning the truth in love;
may they be concerned to care for others;
and may they acquire a true sense of values.
We ask this through Christ our Lord. AMEN.

c) Father of Wisdom,
enlighten by your Holy Spirit all who teach and all who
learn in this class.
May they be led to know Jesus,
who came to teach life in all its fullness.

May they bring to the world the knowledge of your truth,
and a concern for the good of all people.
We ask this through Christ our Lord. AMEN.

d) Father of Wisdom,
bless all in this class as they continue their studies.
May they be set free from all that would hinder their
search for truth.
Grant them an enthusiasm for exploring the wonderful
world of knowledge.
Preserve in them the sense of wonder at the marvels of
life.
Teach them to discern good from evil.
And make them always thankful for what they have been
given.
We ask this through Christ our Lord. AMEN.

e) Loving God,
bless all in this class as they continue their studies.
Bless all children everywhere
especially those who are deprived.
We pray for those who suffer from poverty or illness,
that they may be delivered from misery and fear.
We ask this through Christ our Lord. AMEN.

f) God of Compassion,
we pray your blessings on all teachers,
who follow in the steps of Jesus Christ;
inspire them with concern for every aspect of the life of
their pupils,
as they help them grow in wisdom, age and grace.
We ask this through Christ our Lord. AMEN.

May almighty God bless you,
the Father, and the Son, ✱ and the Holy Spirit. AMEN.

FOR ONE GOING TO SEA

A reading from the Book of Job   *38:8-11*

From the heart of the tempest the Lord gave Job his
    answer.
He said:
Who pent up the sea behind closed doors
    when it leapt tumultuous out of the womb,
when I wrapped it in a robe of mist
    and made black clouds its swaddling bands;
when I marked the bounds it was not to cross
    and made it fast with a bolted gate?
Come thus far, I said, and no farther:
    here your proud waves shall break.

Responsorial Psalm   *Ps 10*

R   GIVE THANKS TO THE LORD FOR HIS LOVE IS
      EVERLASTING.

1. Some sailed to the sea in ships
   to trade on the mighty waters.
   These men have seen the Lord's deeds,
   the wonders he does in the deep. R

2. For he spoke; he summoned the gale,
   tossing the waves of the sea
   up to heaven and back into the deep;
   their souls melted away in their distress. R

3. They staggered, reeled like drunkards,
   for all their skill was gone.
   Then they cried to the Lord in their need
   and he rescued them in their distress. R

4. He stilled the storm to a whisper;
   all the waves of the sea were hushed.
   They rejoiced because of the calm
   and he led them to the haven they desired. R

A reading from the holy Gospel according to Mark.

4:35:41

With the coming of evening, Jesus said to his disciples, 'Let us cross over to the other side'. And leaving the crowd behind they took him, just as he was, in the boat; and there were other boats with him. Then it began to blow a gale and the waves were breaking into the boat so that it was almost swamped. But he was in the stern, his head on the cushion, asleep. They woke him and said to him, 'Master, do you not care? We are going down!' And he woke up and rebuked the wind and said to the sea, 'Quiet now! Be calm!' And the wind dropped, and all was calm again. Then he said to them, 'Why are you so frightened? How is it that you have no faith?' They were filled with awe and said to one another, 'Who can this be? Even the wind and the sea obey him.'

Let us pray:

For a woman:

Lord, pour out your blessing on N,
about to go out to sea.
Protect her against all dangers:
give her joy in the vision of your mighty works,
and make her voyage profitable.
We ask this through Christ our Lord.

For a man:
Lord, pour out your blessing on N,
about to go out to sea.
Protect him against all dangers:
give him joy in the vision of your mighty works,
and make his voyage profitable.
We ask this through Christ our Lord.

We pray to God for all seafarers
as they go about their daily calling:
we pray for all who assist them,
the keepers of lights, the pilots of ports,
and those who are in charge of the lifeboats.
Grant them your strength and protection,
and be with them in every need.
We ask this through Christ our Lord. AMEN.

May almighty God bless you,
the Father, and the Son, ✠ and the Holy Spirit.
AMEN.

A SEPARATED PERSON

Let us listen to the word of God.

(One or more of the following passages may be chosen.)

---

a) St Paul reminds us of the Lord's word to him:
'My grace is enough for you:
for power is at full stretch in weakness.' *2 Corinthians 12:9*

or

b) Peter went up to Jesus and said:
'Lord, how often must I forgive my brother if he wrongs me?
As often as seven times?'
Jesus answered:
'Not seven, I tell you, but seventy-seven times!'

Matthew 18:21-22

or

c) St Paul prayed:
That I may come to know Christ and the power of his resurrection, and partake of his sufferings. *Philippians 3:10*

or

d) The Psalmist sings:
O Lord, you search me and you know me,
you know my resting and my rising,
you discern my purpose from afar.

You mark when I walk or lie down,
All my ways lie open to you.   *Psalm 138:1-3*

Let us pray for God's blessing on N

Compassionate God,
send your blessing on N,
who feels so helpless, so without hope.
You decreed our days before we came into being.
Help N to see the ways of your love,
and the purpose and direction of the life you have
    given.
Fill us all with trust in you
and with the courage we need
to support each other in times of trial.
Give N healing for all hurts
and the grace of forgiveness.
Enable us always to be thankful
for all the good things life has given us.
We praise and bless you through Jesus Christ our
    Lord. AMEN.

N, may almighty God bless you,
the Father, and the Son, ✠ and the Holy Spirit.
AMEN.

A SHIP OR BOAT

In St Mark's Gospel we read:

With the coming of evening that same day, Jesus said
to his disciples: 'Let us cross over to the other side.' And
leaving the crowd behind they took him, just as he was,
in the boat; and there were other boats with him. Then
it began to blow a great gale and the waves were breaking
into the boat so that it was almost swamped. But he was
in the stern, his head on the cushion, asleep. They woke
him and said to him, 'Master, do you not care? We are
lost!' And he woke up and rebuked the wind and said
to the sea, 'Quiet now! Be calm!' And the wind dropped,
and there followed a great calm. Then he said to them,
'Why are you so frightened? Have you still no faith?'
They were overcome with awe and said to one another,
'Who can this be? Even the wind and the sea obey him.'

Mark 4:35-41

Responsorial Psalm   *Ps 106*

R   THEY CRIED TO THE LORD AND HE RESCUED THEM.

1. Some sailed to the sea in ships
    to trade on the mighty waters.
    These men have seen the Lord's deeds,
    the wonders he does in the deep. R

2. For he spoke; he summoned the gale,
    tossing the waves of the sea.
    Then they cried to the Lord in their need
    and he rescued them in their distress. R

3. He stilled the storm to a whisper:
    all the waves of the sea were hushed.

They rejoiced because of the calm
and he led them to the haven they desired. R

4. Let them thank the Lord for his love,
for the wonders he does for his people.
Let them exalt him in the gathering of the people
and praise him in the meeting of the elders. R

Let us pray:

Lord God,
ruler of the universe,
bless this ship/boat ✠
and all who will sail in it.
Reward those who have laboured in its building.
Protect it in fair weather and foul,
and bring it to peaceful harbours
when the voyage is done.

Protect all seafarers in the duties and dangers of their calling.
Bless all who work to make safe the seaways,
and all who work in the rescue services.

Let the blessing of your peace be upon us all,
through the merits of Jesus Christ, our Lord.
AMEN

May Almighty God bless you all,
the Father, and the Son, ✠ and the Holy Spirit.
AMEN.

PARENTS OF A SICK CHILD

In the Gospel according to St Luke we read:

A man named Jairus fell at Jesus' feet and pleaded with
him to come to his house, because he had an only
daughter about twelve years old, who was dying. Jesus
spoke to the man, 'Do not be afraid, only have faith and
she will be saved.'   *Luke 8:41.50*

Lord, bless the parents of N
who come to you in their need.
They are thankful for all the time
when their child was strong and healthy.
They take comfort from the love
you have always shown to children:
remembering how you restored to life
the son of the widow of Nain
and the daughter of Jairus.

Give them courage to hide their worry and anxiety
as they try to soothe their child's pain.
Let them see that in this illness
they can come closer to you and to one another.
We join with them in praying with all our hearts
that you may heal their child.
Grant each of us the grace to say at all times,
'Welcome to your holy will'.
We make our prayer through Christ our Lord.
AMEN.

VISITS TO A SICK CHILD

INTRODUCTION:

Let the children come to me; do not keep them back from me.

The following readings, prayers and blessings will help the minister to pray with sick children and their families. They are provided as an example of what can be done and may be adapted as necessary. The minister may wish to invite those present to prepare for the reading from scripture, perhaps by a brief introduction or through a moment of silence.

If the child does not already know the minister, the latter should seek to establish a friendly and easy relationship with the child. Therefore, the greeting which begins the visit should be an informal one.

The minister should help sick children to understand that the sick are very special in the eyes of God because they are suffering as Christ suffered and because they can offer their sufferings for the salvation of the world.

In praying with the sick child the minister chooses, together with the child and the family if possible, suitable elements of common prayer in the form of a brief liturgy of the Word. This may consist of a reading from scripture, simple one-line prayers taken from scripture which can be repeated by the child, other familiar prayers such as the Lord's Prayer, the Hail Mary, litanies, or a simple form of the general intercessions. The laying on of hands may be added by the priest, if appropriate, after the child has been blessed.

OUTLINE OF THE RITE

Reading
Responsory
The Lord's Prayer
Concluding prayer
Blessing

Reading

One of the following readings may be used for a brief liturgy of the Word. Other readings may be chosen, for example: Mark 5:21-23, 35-43, Jesus raises the daughter of Jairus and gives her back to her parents; Mark 9:14-27, Jesus cures a boy and gives him back to his father; Luke 7:11-15, Jesus raises a young man, the only son of his mother, and gives him back to her; John 4:46-53, Jesus gives his second sign by healing an official's son. In addition, other stories concerning the Lord's healing ministry may be found suitable, especially if told with the simplicity and clarity of one of the children's versions of Scripture.

a) **A reading from the holy Gospel according to Mark.**
9:33-37

Jesus proposes the child as the ideal of those who would enter the kingdom.

Jesus and his disciples came to Capernaum, and when Jesus was in the house he asked the disciples, 'What were you arguing about on the road?' They said nothing because they had been arguing which of them was the greatest. So he sat down, called the Twelve to him and said, 'If anyone wants to be first, he must make himself

184

last of all and servant of all.' He then took a little child, set him in front of them, put his arms around him, and said to them, 'Anyone who welcomes one of these little children in my name, welcomes me; and anyone who welcomes me welcomes not me but the one who sent me.' This is the Gospel of the Lord.

b) A reading from the holy Gospel according to Mark.

10:13-16

Jesus welcomes the children and lays his hands on them.

People were bringing little children to Jesus, for him to touch them. The disciples turned them away, but when Jesus saw this he was indignant and said to them, 'Let the little children come to me; do not stop them; for it is to such as these that the kingdom of God belongs. I tell you solemnly, anyone who does not welcome the kingdom of God like a little child will never enter it.' Then he put his arms around them, laid his hands on them and gave them his blessing.
This is the Gospel of the Lord.

Responsory

After the reading of the word of God, time may be set apart for silent reflection if the child is capable of this form of prayer. The minister should also explain the meaning of the reading to those present, adapting it to their circumstances.

The minister may then help the child and the family to respond to the word of God. The following short responsory may be used:

Jesus, come to me.
R   JESUS, COME TO ME.

Jesus, put your hand on me.

R JESUS, PUT YOUR HAND ON ME.

Jesus bless me.

R JESUS, BLESS ME.

The Lord's Prayer

The minister introduces the Lord's Prayer in these or similar words:

Let us pray to the Father using those words which Jesus himself used:

All say:

Our Father ...

Concluding prayer

The minister says a concluding prayer. One of the following may be used:

a) God of love,
   ever caring,
   ever strong,
   stand by us in our time of need.
   Watch over your child N who is sick,
   look after him/her in every danger,
   and grant him/her your healing and peace.

   We ask this in the name of Jesus the Lord.
   R AMEN.

b) Father,
   in your love
   you gave us Jesus
   to help us rise triumphant over grief and pain.

Look on your child N who is sick
and see in his/her sufferings those of your Son.

Grant N a share in the strength you granted
your Son that he/she too may be a sign
of your goodness, kindness, and loving care.

We ask this in the name of Jesus the Lord.

R AMEN.

Blessing

The minister makes a sign of the cross on the
child's forehead, saying one of the following:

a) N, when you were baptised,
you were marked with the cross of Jesus.
I (we) make this cross ✠ on your forehead
and ask the Lord to bless you,
and restore you to health.

R AMEN.

or

b) All praise and glory is yours, heavenly God,
for you have called us to serve you in love.
Have mercy on us and listen to our prayer
as we ask you to help N.

Bless ✠ your beloved child,
and restore him/her to health
in the name of Jesus the Lord.

R AMEN.

Each one present may in turn trace the sign of
the cross on the child's forehead, in silence.

If the minister is a priest or deacon, he
concludes:

**May the blessing of almighty God,
the Father, and the Son, ✠ and the Holy Spirit,
come upon you and remain with you for ever.**

R AMEN.

The priest may then lay hands upon the sick
child, in silence. A minister who is not a priest
or deacon invokes God's blessing and makes the
sign of the cross on himself or herself, while
saying:

**May the Lord bless us,
protect us from all evil,
and bring us to everlasting life.**

R AMEN.

FOR SPORTING EVENTS

The Apostle Paul reminded the Corinthians that they belonged in a special way to God. He urged them to 'use your bodies for God's glory.' He said 'Don't you know that your body is the temple of the Holy Spirit?' Through the words of Paul we acknowledge that our bodies are a great gift through which we can show the glory of God in music, art, dance and sport.

Let us pray:

Lord God,
we thank you for continuing health of mind and body.
We thank you also for good sporting competition and for success and failure when they come our way. Help us to compete to the fullness of our abilities but not to make winning at all costs the pinnacle of our ambition.
If we achieve success may we accept it with gratitude.
Comfort us with the realisation that it is often on the anvil of failure that true character is moulded and shaped.

We make our prayer through Christ our Lord. AMEN.

THROATS, ON ST BLAISE'S DAY

The candles to be used for the blessing of throats
are blessed on the day before the memorial of St
Blaise. The appropriate Scripture readings for the
Mass may be used if the blessing takes place
outside of Mass. These readings are Romans 5:1-5;
Psalm 116; the Response is Mark 16:15; the Gospel
is Mark 16:15-20.

Our help is in the name of the Lord.
R   WHO MADE HEAVEN AND EARTH.
Let us pray:

Almighty and merciful God,
you sent your Word, through whom you created all things,
to renew that creation by his incarnation.

For his faith in Jesus Christ, true God and true man, your
martyr and bishop, St Blaise,
patiently endured suffering and death.

Supported by his merits and prayers
we ask you to bless ✠ these candles
so that all afflicted with ailments of the throat
may feel your healing power in their lives,
and, blessing your holy name,
may give thanks and praise to you,
who with your Son, Jesus Christ,
in the unity of the Holy Spirit, lives and reigns for ever.
AMEN.

The candles are sprinkled with blessed water.

Using two crossed and unlighted candles the minister touches the throat of each person, saying:

Through the intercession of St Blaise, bishop and martyr, may God deliver you from all ailments of the throat and from every other evil:
In the name of the Father, ✠ and of the Son, and of the Holy Spirit. AMEN.

Grant this through our Lord, Jesus Christ, your Son, who lives and reigns with you and the Holy Spirit, one God, for ever and ever.
AMEN.

STILLBORN BABY

When Mary greeted her cousin Elizabeth
Elizabeth replied:
'The moment your greeting reached my ears,
the child in my womb leapt for joy.'   *Luke 1:44*

John the Baptist, born in joy to his mother
in her old age would die a cruel death.

Let us pray:

God, the giver of life,
help this mother
who knew the life of her baby within her
to understand that her child's life is complete.
Grant that she and her child and her child's father
may all be reunited in your love
when their own lives on earth are ended.
AMEN.

TABLE PRAYERS

GRACE BEFORE MEALS

1.

a) Advent

The eyes of all creatures look to you, O Lord,
to give them their food in due season.
You give it, they gather it up:
you open your hand, they have their fill.

Send victory like a dew, you heavens.
R   LET THE EARTH OPEN AND BRING FORTH OUR
SAVIOUR.

Lord, through your goodness the rain and snow
water the earth, making it bring forth and sprout,
giving seed to the sower and bread to the eater:
so may we be nourished also by your Word,
whose coming we await in hope. AMEN.

b) Christmas

The eyes of all creatures look to you, O Lord,
to give them their food in due season.
You give it, they gather it up:
you open your hand, they have their fill.

Unto us a child is born.
R   UNTO US A SON IS GIVEN!

Lord, the goodness and kindness of our Saviour has
appeared. We thank you for the salvation he has
brought, and for these gifts which we share in unity
with him who reigns with you for ever. AMEN.

The eyes of all creatures look to you, O Lord,
to give them their food in due season.
You give it, they gather it up:
you open your hand, they have their fill.

A pure heart create for me, O Lord.
R GIVE ME AGAIN THE JOY OF YOUR HELP.

Lord, in this time of prayer and fasting may we
learn to share our bread with the hungry and needy,
so as to receive the reward promised to all who see
in the needy the face of your Son, Jesus Christ, our
Lord. AMEN.

The eyes of all creatures look to you, O Lord,
to give them their food in due season.
You give it, they gather it up:
you open your hand, they have their fill.

Rejoice and be glad, alleluia.
R THE LORD IS RISEN INDEED, ALLELUIA.

Lord God, as we share in the joy of Christ's
resurrection, fill us with your Spirit, that we may
share our food in peace and love. We ask this
through Christ, our Lord. AMEN.

The eyes of all creatures look to you, O Lord,
to give them their food in due season.
You give it, they gather it up:
you open your hand, they have their fill.

Bless the Lord, my soul!
R LORD GOD, HOW GREAT YOU ARE.

Lord God, you provide for all our needs.
Teach us to share our food in simplicity and
thankfulness.
Make us always mindful of the poor and needy
and bring us to your heavenly table:
through Christ our Lord. AMEN.

2.

Bless us, O God, as we sit together.
Bless the food we eat today.
Bless the hands that made the food.
Bless us, O God. AMEN.

3.

Blessed be our Lord Jesus Christ
who shared the loaves and fishes with the five
thousand.
May the blessing of God be upon our meal
and upon our sharing in food and friendship.

(From the Irish)

4.

Bless, O Lord, this food we are about to eat.
May it benefit us in body and soul.
As you, Lord, have shared your blessings with us,
may we be willing to share our food
with any creature in need this day.   *(From the Irish)*

5.

Bless us, O Lord, and these thy gifts,
which of thy bounty we are about to receive,
through Christ our Lord. AMEN.

6

At a wedding

Let us bless the Lord this day;
bless him who makes the earth fruitful
giving bread to strengthen our lives
and wine to cheer our hearts.

As we share his gifts at this table
may he bless N and N,
their families and all their friends.
May we all come together again
at the great wedding banquet in the kingdom of
God,
as one family through Jesus Christ our Lord. AMEN.

7.

For Christmas dinner

Parent:

Blessed are you, God our Father,
you have gathered us together once more at this
Christmas table.
Christ is the light that shone in our darkness.
May the light of that first Christmas night
shine on our table and on all in our house.
(The mother may light the table candles at this
time).
God, you are the giver of all good gifts.
We thank you for this Christmas feast,
for the beauty of decoration, for the food upon the
table,
for all who have worked to prepare it,
and for keeping us together today and throughout
the year.
(If there are visitors:

We thank you for the presence of our friends
and ask you to bless them.)
May your blessing be upon us all
in the name of the Father, and of the Son, ✠ and of
     the Holy Spirit. AMEN.

GRACE AFTER MEALS

1.

We give thee thanks, O almighty God, for all thy
     benefits:
who live and reign for ever and ever. AMEN.
May the souls of the faithful departed
through the mercy of God rest in peace. AMEN.

2.

Thank you, God, for the food we have eaten.
Thank you, God, for all our friends.
Thank you, God, for everything. AMEN.

3.

All praise to the most generous God,
all praise to the King of heaven,
all praise to Jesus Christ
for the food that has refreshed us.
May he who has given us this food on earth,
grant us eternal food in heaven. AMEN.

(From the Irish)

4.

Unending thanks to you, all-powerful God, who
     have given us these gifts.

May the God of heaven and his Son, Jesus Christ,
protect us against all who would do us any harm.
May he who gave us this food for the body
grant us a fine day,
a life without sin or shame,
the timely sacraments,
a good death and eternal food in heaven. AMEN.

(From the Irish)

TEACHERS OF THE YOUNG

St Paul writes to Timothy:

Keep as your pattern the sound teaching you have heard
from me, in the faith and love that are in Christ Jesus.
With the help of the Holy Spirit who dwells in us, look
after that precious thing taken in trust.

2 Timothy 1:13-14

Let us pray for God's blessing on N,
who like Jesus is called teacher.

For a woman:

Lord, pour out your Holy Spirit on N,
privileged to work with the young.
May all her work with them
be marked with respect and sensitivity.
Teach her to show these young people their own
    worth,
and to reveal your love for them.
Through her words and example
may she bring them closer to you.
We ask this through Christ our Lord.
AMEN.

For a man:

Lord, pour out your Holy Spirit on N,
privileged to work with the young.
May all his work with them
be marked with respect and sensitivity.

Teach him to show these young people their own
    worth,
and to reveal your love for them.
Through his words and example
may he bring them closer to you.
We ask this through Christ our Lord.
AMEN.

N, may almighty God bless you,
the Father, and the Son, ✠ and the Holy Spirit.
    AMEN.

TRANSIENTS/THE HOMELESS

A reading from the Book of Deuteronomy   *26:5-9*

Moses said to the people:

In the sight of the Lord your God, you must make this
pronouncement:
'My father was a wandering Aramaean. He went down into
Egypt to find refuge there, few in numbers; but there he
became a nation, great, mighty, and strong. The Egyptians
ill-treated us, they gave us no peace and inflicted harsh
slavery on us. But we called on the Lord, the God of our
fathers. The Lord heard our voice and saw our misery, our
toil and our oppression; and the Lord brought us out of
Egypt with mighty hand and outstretched arm, with great
terror, and with signs and wonders. He brought us here
and gave us this land, a land where milk and honey flow.'

Let us pray:

Father of all,
we give into your keeping all who are homeless in
          this land.
Give them your protection on their way,
grant them peace,
and allow them to be accepted by all who meet
          them.
Keep them from illness and accidents;
watch over all the children of the homeless.
We ask this through Christ our Lord. AMEN.

All-loving God,
give to all who use our streets
a good sense of courtesy and cheerfulness to those in
need.

Preserve the homeless from all dangers
and from grave illness or sudden death.
Give them courage to meet opposition
and patience to put up with trials.
Bring them at last to be with you
where there is an end of wandering
and our pilgrimage is finished.
We ask this through Christ our Lord. AMEN.

May the blessing of God Almighty,✠
the Father, the Son, and the Holy Spirit, rest upon
          you;
may he give light to guide you,
courage to support you,
and love to unite you,
now and forever. AMEN.

VEHICLES

God saw all he had made,
and indeed it was very good.   *Genesis 1:31*

Let us pray:

God, our Father,
you have called us to share in your work of
        creation.
We ask your blessing ✠ upon this....
and upon all who will use it.
May they travel in safety to their journey's end.
We make this prayer through Christ our Lord.
AMEN.

        For the owner of a car/motorhome etc.

Father, may N see in this ....
the possibilities of service.
May he/she travel with care,
with consideration for his/her neighbour.

Lord, hear our prayer.

A WIDOW OR WIDOWER

Our Lord Jesus Christ experienced loneliness and separation. In the desolation of Gethsemane he cried out that his suffering might pass. On the Cross he asked the Father why he had been so forsaken.

The loss of the physical presence of a marriage partner is indeed a painful experience. But each can truly say with St John Chrysostom: 'Those whom we love and lose are no longer where they were before. They are now wherever we are.'

Let us listen to the comforting words of Our Lord in St John's Gospel:

Jesus said:
Let not your hearts be troubled;
believe in God, believe also in me.
In my Father's house are many rooms;
if it were not so, would I have told you
that I go to prepare a place for you?
And when I go and prepare a place for you,
I will come again and will take you to myself,
that where I am you may be also.

John 14:1-3

Let us pray:

For a widow:
Eternal God and Father,
whose love is stronger than death,
look with pity on our sister whose marriage was a figure

of the union of Christ with his Church.
She is desolate now without the companion
you gave her in that holy sacrament.
Comfort her with your presence
and the indwelling of your Holy Spirit.
Keep her in the joyful hope
of one day being reunited with her loved one
in your heavenly dwelling place.

We ask this through Christ our Lord.

For a widower:

Eternal God and Father,
whose love is stronger than death,
look with pity on our brother whose marriage was
    a figure
of the union of Christ with his Church.
He is desolate now without the companion
you gave him in that holy sacrament.
Comfort him with your presence
and the indwelling of your Holy Spirit.
Keep him in the joyful hope
of one day being reunited with his loved one
in your heavenly dwelling place.

BLESSING

May the blessing of almighty God,
the Father, the Son, ✠ and the Holy Spirit,
rest upon you;
may he give light to guide you,

courage to support you,
and love to unite you,
now and for evermore. AMEN.

WOMEN

'Yes, Lord,' Martha said, 'I believe that you are the Christ, the Son of God, the one who was to come into this world.' When she had said this, she went and called her sister Mary, saying in a low voice, 'The Master is here and wants to see you.'   *John 11:27-28*

Let us pray:

O Holy One, we thank and praise you for the wonder and mystery of womanhood.

We pray that the Christian Church may increasingly value the contribution which women can make to enrich our life as the people of God.

We pray that you, the women of today, will proclaim your faith in Christ in all that you do and say and, in so doing, will draw your sisters and brothers into a closer relationship with him and with one another.

May God grant you the confidence to stand up for what is right, the generosity which makes allowances for human frailty and the love which is always ready to go the second mile. We make this prayer through the one who invites us to follow him, Jesus Christ our Lord. AMEN.

WOMEN ALONE
(SINGLE WOMEN, WIDOWS, DESERTED WIVES ETC.)

Esther beseeched the God of Israel in these words:

'Come to my help, for I am alone and have no one but you, Lord.'

Esther 4:17

Jesus said:

This is my commandment: 'Love one another as I have loved you.'

John 15:12

Let us remember before God those women who have to carry responsibility alone — those caring for elderly relatives, those who are bringing up a family on their own and those who live alone or who have no close family.

God of all comfort and consolation, may your daughters be strengthened and supported by knowing that you have a special love and care for those who have no family to rely on. We pray that they may be blessed with loyal friends who will show your love for them in human terms, rejoicing with them when they rejoice and weeping with them when they weep. We pray in the name of your Son who came into the world alone and who was comforted by the human love of those whom you gave him, Jesus our friend and brother. AMEN.

FOR WORLD PEACE

Jesus said:

'Peace I bequeath to you;
my own peace I give to you;
a peace which the world cannot give,
this is my own gift to you.
Do not let your hearts be troubled or afraid.'

John 14:27

Let us pray:

Eternal God,
creator of the world,
you establish the order which governs all the ages.
Hear our prayer and give us peace in our time
that we may rejoice in your mercy
and praise you without end.

We ask this through Christ our Lord. AMEN.

May the peace of God which passes all understanding
keep your hearts and your minds in Christ Jesus. AMEN.

LEADERS OF YOUTH GROUPS AND ACTIVITIES

Let us listen to the words of Scripture:
They had been arguing which of them was the greatest. So
Jesus sat down, called the Twelve
to him and said,

'If anyone wants to be first, he must make
himself last of all and servant of all.'

He then took a little child whom he set
among them and embraced, and he said to them,

'Anyone who welcomes a little child such as this
in my name, welcomes me; and anyone who welcomes me,
welcomes not me but the one who sent me.'

Mark 9:34-37

Let us pray:

[That we will, like Jesus,
exercise leadership with
service and that, as his
disciples, we will care
deeply for the young people
entrusted to us on this evening.]
(Pause for silent prayer)

God, our Father,
We thank you for the joy and privilege
of working with and for our young people
who are so infinitely precious to you.
Help us, through the power of the Holy Spirit,

to exercise leadership with service,
and thus become more faithful disciples of Jesus
        your Son,
who is Lord forever and ever, AMEN.

INDEX

Other Prayer Books
from Servant Publications

Draw Me
Catholic Prayers for Every Occasion in a Woman's Life
Carmen Rojas

Draw Me is a personal prayer book, designed to address the varied need of a woman. It includes prayers of faith and forgiveness; prayers for husbands, children and friends; prayers for overcoming depression, grief and loneliness; and traditional Catholic prayers and devotions. A special section includes morning and evening prayers, the rosary, the stations of the cross and prayers to help you prepare for confession and communion.   **$7.99**

Your Family Prayer Book
An Easy Way to Pray Together Every Day
Carmen Rojas

Your Family Prayer Book addresses the challenges of everyday life by providing families with a simple pattern of prayer that can be used every day, seasonally, or just on special occasions. Each entry includes a short psalm reading, another Scripture and three brief intercessions—all listed on the same page. Here is a prayer book for modern Catholic families of all shapes and sizes.   **$7.99**

Available at your Christian bookstore or from:
**Servant Publications • Dept. 209 • P.O. Box 7455
Ann Arbor, Michigan 48107**
Please include payment plus $1.25 per book
for postage and handling.
*Send for our FREE catalog of Christian
books, music, and cassettes.*